Introduction

The Book

My interest in drumming started when I was three-years old. I discovered some wooden forks and spoons in a kitchen drawer and proceeded to bang away on every pot, pan and Tupperware container that I could find.

My mom probably should have immediately gone out and bought me drumsticks and a mini-drumset. After all, I ended up destroying all of her wooden utensils and Tupperware! What kept my mother from buying such a toy? What keeps many parents from buying mini-drumsets for their young, would-be percussionists?

Parents often feel conflicted when they think about going out to buy these toy sets for their children. These instruments are expensive and normally offer only a quick fix to the child. Youngsters bash away on the drums for a few days or weeks at a time and soon get bored. As with many toys, the item ends up stored in a closet or the garage or gets taken to the nearest charity drop-off box.

This teaching guide is designed for parents/teachers of two to six year-olds, who want to increase the quality and extend the life of the mini-drumset experience. Combine the activities in this book with a drum kit (and a few other odds and ends mentioned in the book), and an inspiring method is born.

Since most children this age are not necessarily ready to learn how to play-along to their parent's favorite Rush, Dream Theatre, and Frank Zappa songs, *Drumset for Preschoolers* focuses on the development of early childhood and general music skills. The mini-drumset becomes less of a toy and more of a learning tool.

After only a short time using this teaching method, parents/teachers will find that their investment in a small drumset was well worth it. For the young drum student, there's nothing like combining learning with fun. He/she will be beaming from ear to ear.

Speaking of ears, if volume is a concern, don't worry. When you read ahead, you'll see that this method takes this issue into account. It is possible to use a drum kit as a great educational tool without causing family headaches.

Note: *This book will also work well with young people and adults with mild to moderate learning disabilities.*

Drummer on Front Cover: Steven Sanford

Many Types of

Drumset for Preschoolers is designed to work with three-, four-, and five-piece mini- drumsets made by a myriad of manufacturers. Keep in mind that these kits come in a wide range of quality. By spending a little bit more money, you will provide the youngster with a more rewarding playing (and learning) experience.

Full-size drumsets can also be used with smaller drummers. By acquiring a small drum throne (so that the child is comfortable sitting behind the kit), adjusting all of the hardware (hi-hat stand, cymbal stands, rack tom mount, and floor tom legs) as low as possible, and adjusting the angle of the snare drum, rack toms, and floor tom so that each component slopes dramatically towards the small drummer, the bigger drums will work just fine. A good rule of thumb in this case is: the shorter the drummer, the greater the degree that the drums will need to slope towards the player.

The major advantage of a full-size kit is that if the young student stays interested in drumming as 7 or 8 year-olds, a drum kit upgrade won't be necessary. The major disadvantage is that most hi-hat stands are designed only with the adult drummer in mind and are too tall for our purposes here. Also, huge drums can make the young drummer feel slightly intimidated at first glance.

Electronic drumsets are a great alternative to acoustic drums. Though sometimes a bit pricey, these kits are quite adjustable to fit the size of small drummers (though again you may need to purchase an additional small drum throne), don't make much noise unless amplified (headphones would be needed), take up very little space, and often come with special features such a onboard metronomes, thousands of different sounds, an mp3 player port, and comfortable playing surfaces.

The plastic drum kit that comes with the *Rock Band* video game also works seemlessly with this book. Starting with *Rock Band 2* and continuing with *The Beatles: Rock Band* and *Rock Band 3*, a "Freestyle Mode" allows players to use the plastic kit as a stand-alone electronic drumset. In other words, in this mode, when a player hits each pad (or bass drum pedal), drum sounds are produced, and a song from the game does not need to be playing at the same time.

Drumset for Preschoolers also works well as a precursor to the *Rock Band* game itself, especially at the Easy Level. Go to www.andyziker.com for colored drum charts (the same color scheme used in this book) of some of your favorite *Rock Band* songs.

Nevertheless, be cautious about having your youngster overplay on the hard plastic drum pads that make up the *Rock Band* (and *Guitar Hero World Tour*) drumkits. The Ion Rocker by Alesis doubles as a video game controller and real electronic drumset and is much more forgiving on the body. Also, the drum pads from *Rock Band 2* (and beyond) have been designed for more comfortable play.

Table of Contents

Free Supplementary Video Companion

Free supplemental video clips can be found on my website, www.andyziker.com. Designed for parents and teachers without musical training, demonstrations of musical notation will be covered here.

How to Use the Book

Because not all two-year olds have the same ability level, neither do all three-year-olds, etc., labeling of each activity by age is not used. Instead, activities in the book are organized in three levels of complexity, giving the teacher/parent the flexibility to decide where to start their child drummer.

Level 1: Most simple.
Level 2: Slightly more challenging.
Level 3: Even more challenging than Level 2.

Skills/Concepts Covered in the Book

The following is a list of many of the skill/concepts covered in *Drumset for Preschoolers*, throughout the three levels.

Accenting
Alphabet
Alternate Sticking
Back and Forth/One After Another
Beginning /End
Big Endings
Breathing While Performing
Clockwise/Counterclockwise
Coordination
Counting
Playing
Creativity
Crescendos
Discovering Drumset Sounds
Feeling a Pulse
Flat Flams
Foot Technique
Foot/Eye Coordination
Forwards and Backwards
Hand-Eye Coordination
High to Low
In-between-ness
Listening
Numbers
Onomatopoeia
Part of a Whole
Playing in Time
Playing with Music
Rhythmic Reading & Counting Right/Left Hand
Simple Shapes
Slow to Fast
Soft to Loud
Stick Height
Stick Technique
Syllables
Together/Apart

Colored Stickers

For ease in communicating with the young drum student, a color scheme accompanies this teaching manual. (See upcoming section called Color Scheme for the Notes.) To get you started, a page of color stickers (in red, yellow, blue, green and orange) is included as an insert.

The stickers can be placed directly on the drumheads or cymbals of your mini-drumset and/or placed on muffling devices. (See the following section, How to Quiet Down the Drums.) Leftover stickers can be used for rewards.

Note: *Some brands of mini-drumsets come pre-packaged with shape stickers of different colors. These stickers can be just as effective as the ones included in this book and offer the possibility of building shape recognition skills. Be careful, however, about overwhelming the youngster with information overload. Since drumheads have a circular shape, red triangle stickers placed on that drumhead may cause confusion: Is the drumhead a triangle or a circle? Either answer would be correct. When two answers are possible, the learning process can get easily derailed.*

Quieting Down the Drums

A number of companies make mute pads/drum silencers out of neoprene rubber. These add-on devices give you the option to drastically cut down the noise level, but can be a bit pricey.

You can also make your own mute pads out of non-adhesive black shelf liner.
For more on this, go to www.andyziker.com and search for an article called "Homemade Mute Pads." Towels, T-shirts, and other thin pieces of material will also work well. It would be optimal if the colors of these "drum clothes" could match the color-coded system found in the book (see below).

Color Scheme for the Notes

As mentioned previously in the introduction, a company called Harmonix recently created a popular video game called *Rock Band*. In doing so, they instantly and unintentionally standardized colored drumset notation. When the game was created, each of the pads of the *Rock Band* drum controller (corresponding to the scrolling 3-D note chart) was assigned a particular color. Because of this popularity of *Rock Band*, *Drumset for Preschoolers* stays true to the color scheme from the video game.

Below is a drumset key that tells you where each drum or cymbal is placed on the staff (five lines and four spaces), what notehead is used (X's for cymbals and ovals for drums), and what color goes with each part of the drumset.

Note: *If you only have one tom (making up a three-piece drumset), assign blue as the color of that drum, as shown in the next section called Drumset Diagrams. If you have two toms (making up a four-piece drumset), assign yellow for the rack tom (the high tom) and blue for the other tom (normally a floor tom).*

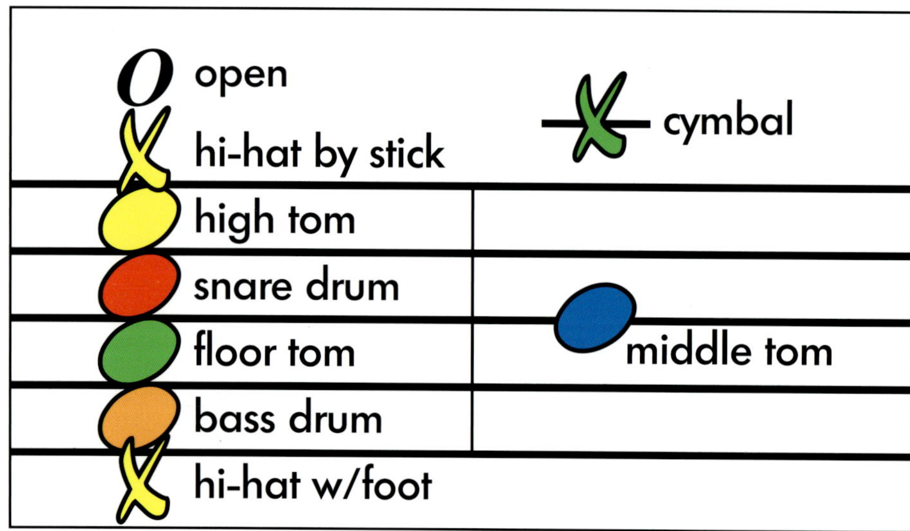

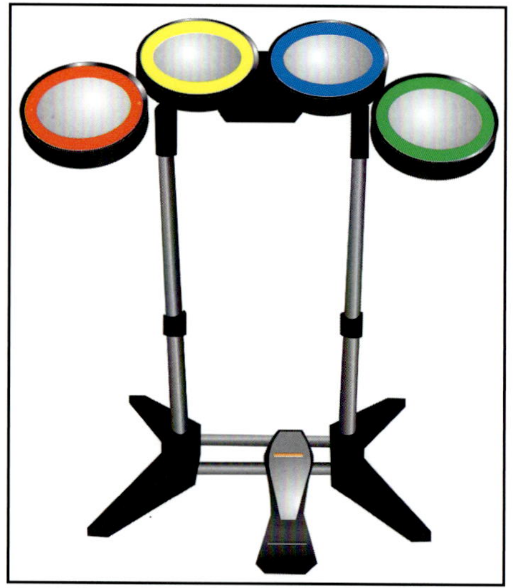

Drumset Diagrams

Most children's (also called junior, kid's, toy, or miniature) drumsets come in one of two configurations. The following diagrams show these two common set-ups from the front and back view. The individual parts of the drumset are labeled, and the color scheme for the stickers is seen in the back view.

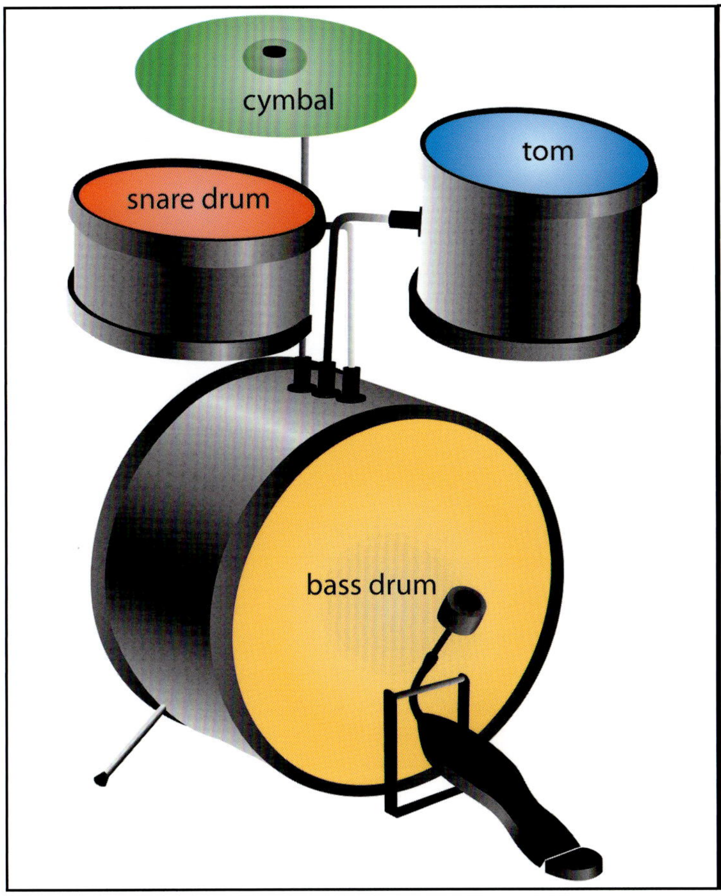

Three-Piece Back View 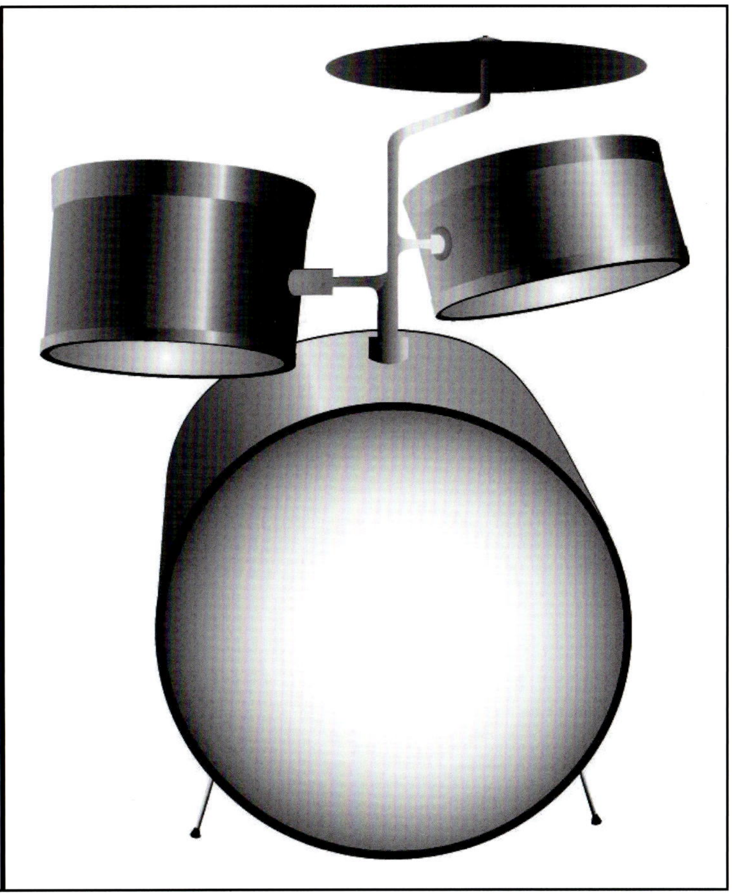 **Three-Piece Front View**

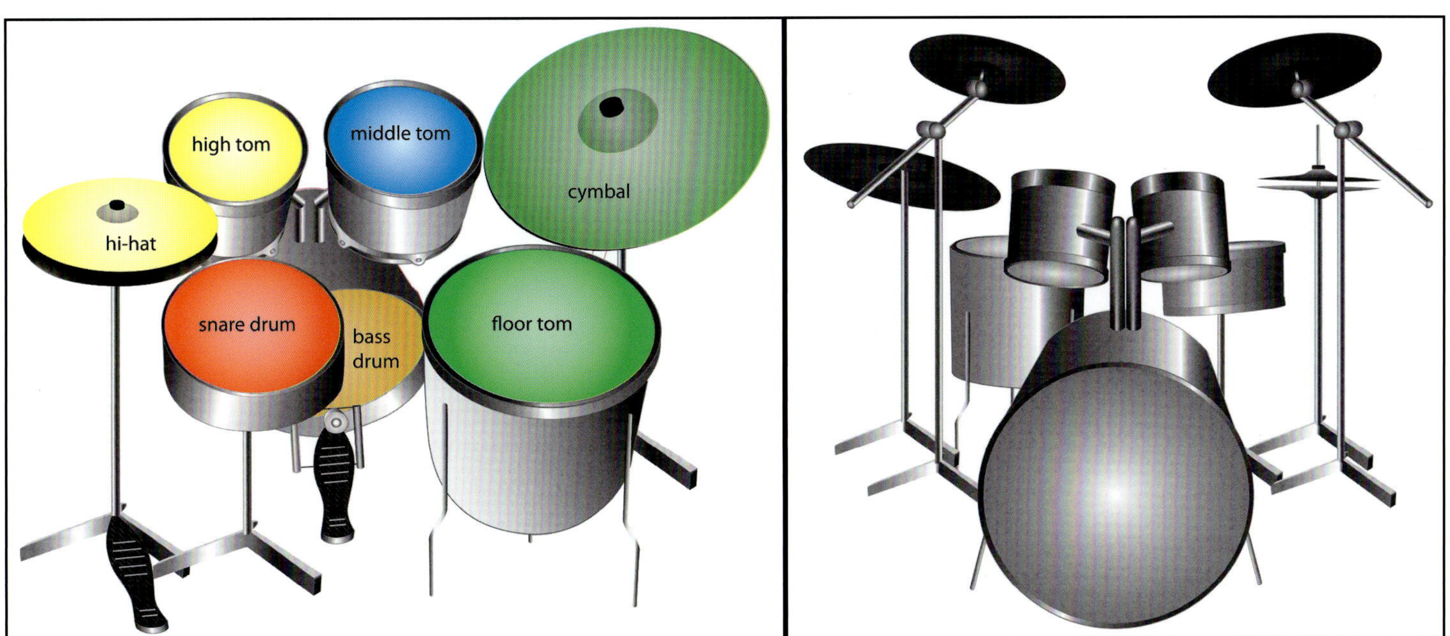

Five-Piece Back View **Five-Piece Front View**

← The *Rock Band* drum kit is shown to the left. The red pad on the left is always assigned a snare drum sound, while the yellow pad is either a high tom or a hi-hat, the blue pad is either a middle tom or a ride cymbal, and the green pad is either a floor tom or a crash cymbal.

How to Set Up and Tune the Drumset

When you take the components out of the box (unless you bought a fully assembled drum kit), carefully lay the parts on the floor in front of you. Don't get discouraged. Follow the instructions found in the following pages. You can do this!

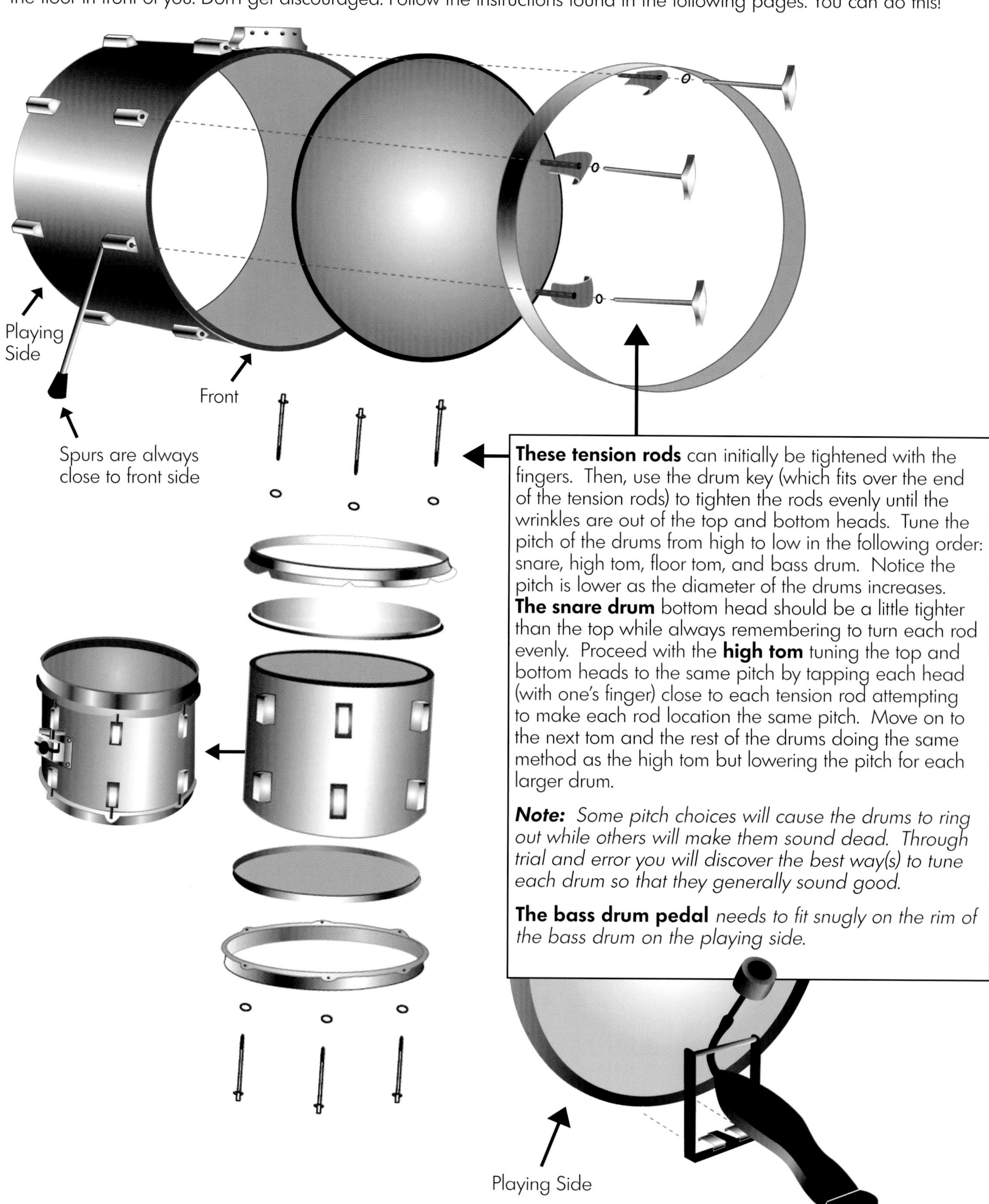

These tension rods can initially be tightened with the fingers. Then, use the drum key (which fits over the end of the tension rods) to tighten the rods evenly until the wrinkles are out of the top and bottom heads. Tune the pitch of the drums from high to low in the following order: snare, high tom, floor tom, and bass drum. Notice the pitch is lower as the diameter of the drums increases. **The snare drum** bottom head should be a little tighter than the top while always remembering to turn each rod evenly. Proceed with the **high tom** tuning the top and bottom heads to the same pitch by tapping each head (with one's finger) close to each tension rod attempting to make each rod location the same pitch. Move on to the next tom and the rest of the drums doing the same method as the high tom but lowering the pitch for each larger drum.

Note: *Some pitch choices will cause the drums to ring out while others will make them sound dead. Through trial and error you will discover the best way(s) to tune each drum so that they generally sound good.*

The bass drum pedal *needs to fit snugly on the rim of the bass drum on the playing side.*

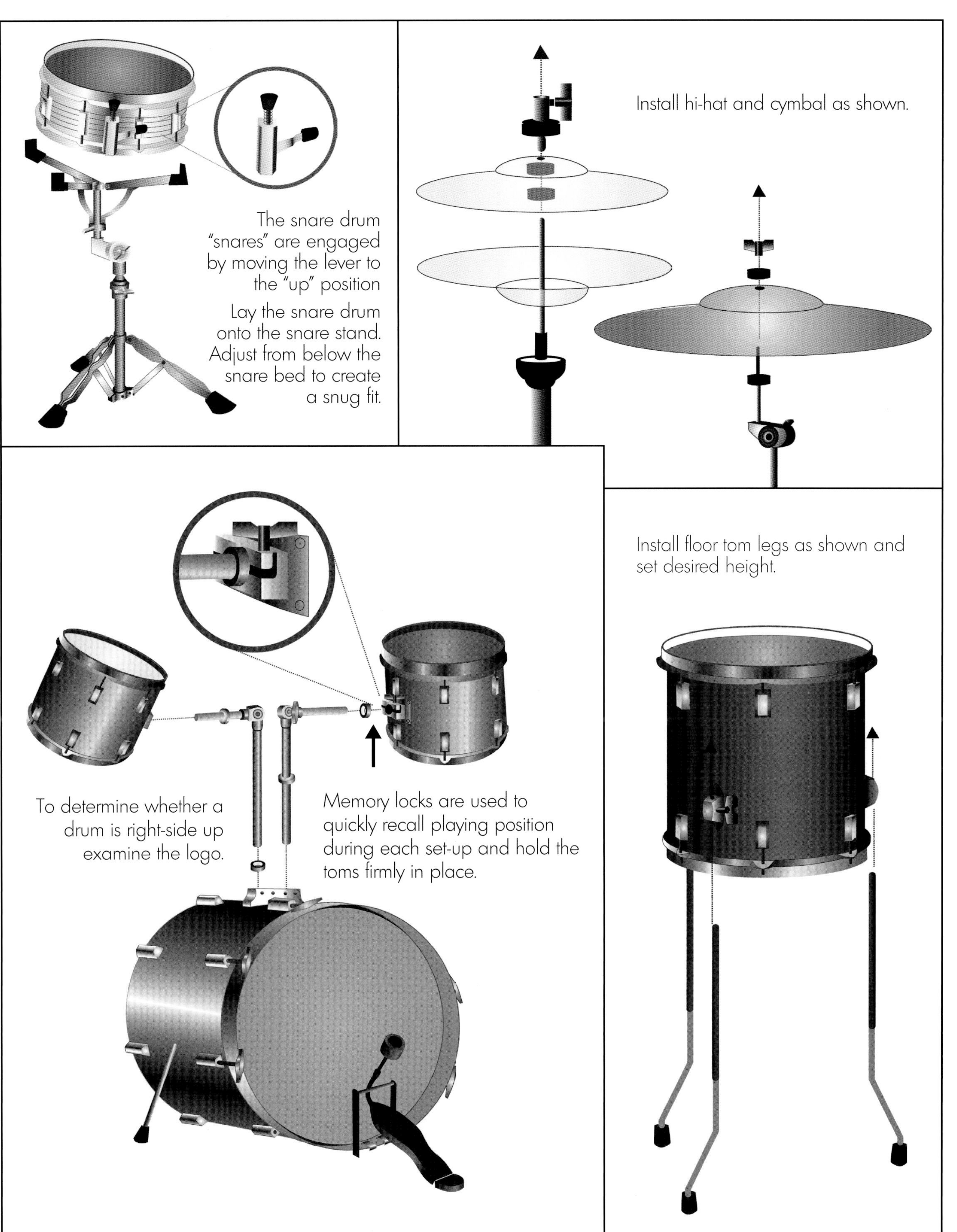

The snare drum
"snares" are engaged
by moving the lever to
the "up" position
Lay the snare drum
onto the snare stand.
Adjust from below the
snare bed to create
a snug fit.
Install hi-hat and cymbal as shown.
To determine whether a
drum is right-side up
examine the logo.
Memory locks are used to
quickly recall playing position
during each set-up and hold the
toms firmly in place.
Install floor tom legs as shown and
set desired height.

Protecting the Hearing of Your Little One

To protect against hearing loss by your child or yourself, consider one of the following three recommendations.

1. Purchase drum mute pads or place towels over the heads and cymbals with a little tape to keep them from sliding off
2. Acquire good headphones to block out harmful frequencies. Search for a comfortable pair that cover the ears and are adjustable to fit the child's head.
3. Stock up on low-cost earplugs that are made of foam (these are available at most music stores) or the form fitting plugs such as Mack's Pillow Soft Earplugs.

Picking Out a Pair of Drumsticks

If you're lucky, you'll receive a free pair of drumsticks with your mini-drumset. If not, "junior" drumsticks are made by a number of stick manufacturers. If you can't find them at your local music store(s), search the many e-commerce sites on the internet.

Young children can also handle using an "adult-length" drumstick, especially a small- diameter stick such as a "7A". They will find it easier to reach the tom(s), hi-hat, and cymbal(s) with these sticks.

How to Hold the Drumsticks

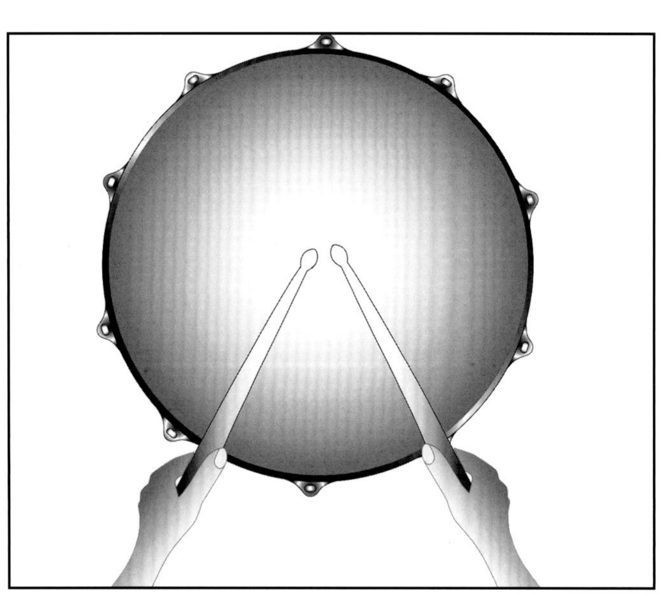

Ready Position:
When playing a drum, it is important to have the sticks and arms form an angle of attack as shown. This allows you to more easily aim at the center of the playing surface in a relaxed fashion. Notice that the sticks become an extension of the arms. The sticks are, in a sense, "shooting out of your arms." The tips of the sticks hover about three inches above the head. You're ready to play!

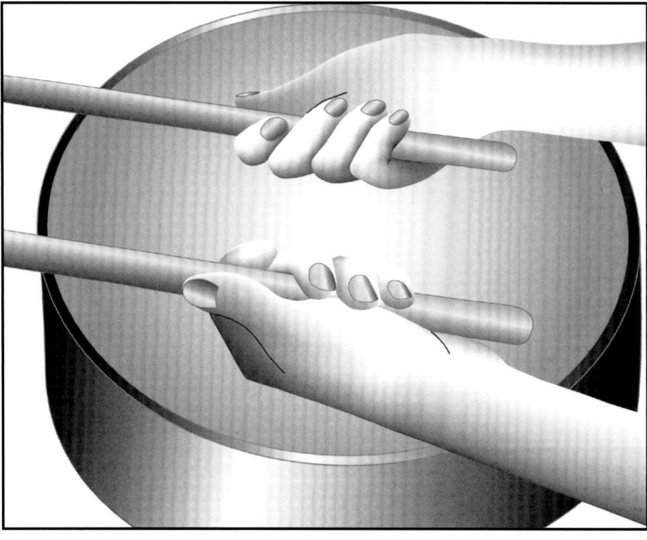

Underside View of Hand Technique:
The flat underside of the thumb makes contact with the stick, while the fingers wrap around naturally. Ideally, there should be some empty space between the thumb and the index finger.

***Note:** Your young student may have a tendency to place their pointer fingers on top of the stick. This is a bad habit to get into. It prevents the stick from bouncing freely off the drumhead. If this becomes engrained, you will need to gently and persistently remind the youngster to tuck their pointer finger back under the stick.*

There are generally two ways to play the pedal(s).

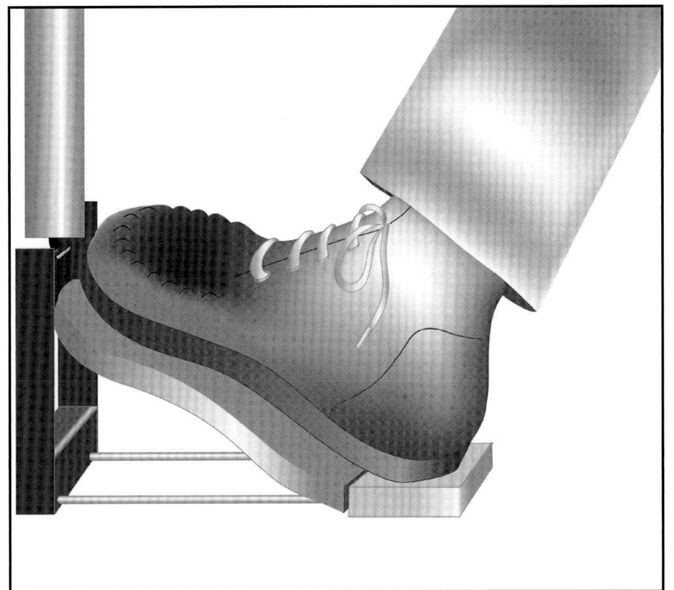

Heel-Down Technique:
Keep the entire foot on the pedal. It's unnecessary to lift the toe portion of your foot off the pedal. The beater comes off the batter head, producing a mellow, ringing tone from the bass drum.

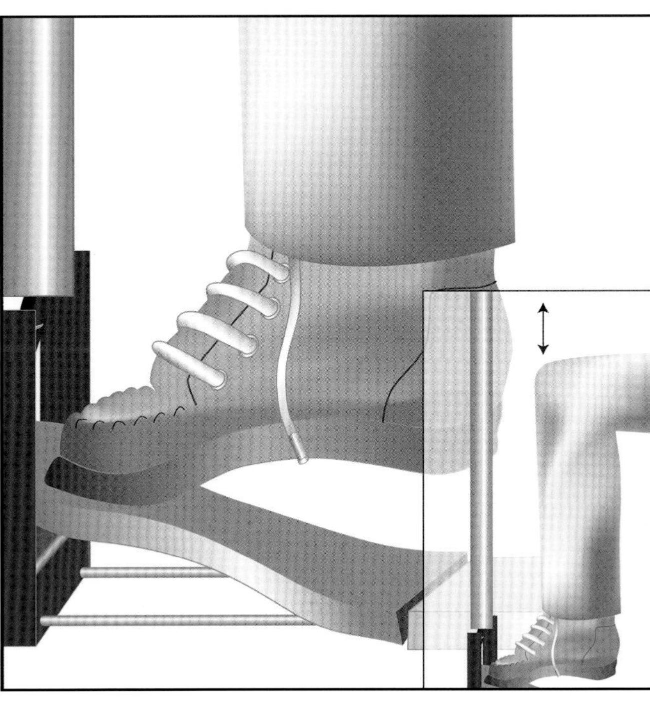

Heel-Up Technique:
Imagine that a puppet master is pulling up at your knee with a string. The heel raises off the pedal, while the ball of your foot remains. The beater normally strikes and stays on the head, creating a muffled tone with loads of attack. However, by dropping the heel back down during attack, the beater comes off the head.

NOTE: *Most young children haven't had much experience manipulating pedals. Their intuition tells them that if they pick their entire foot off the pedal and stomp down with all of their might, they will be able to play louder. Frustration can ensue when they realize that this isn't true. Lifting their foot completely off the pedal will cause a loss of control.*

To help teach good foot pedal technique, kneel down near the bass drum while the student's foot is in on the bass drum pedal. Take your right hand and gently place it on top of their foot or shoe. Push down with a little bit of force and repeat in a rapid succession of notes. The faster you go, the more that the little one will enjoy this. Now have the student try it. Ah! Good foot technique has been achieved!

Level 1

Let's Play Together

Act 1: Have the student sit behind the drumkit, while you sit in a chair right next to or directly across from it. Ask them to play anything they want. Once they are through with their drum solo, or if they don't embrace the idea of improvising, begin to stomp and/or clap a simple beat and have the child respond to it. Allow them to play whatever they want on the drumset while reacting to you. (It is very important to not force the student/child to play a specific beat at this point. Let them feel comfortable within the creative process. If they respond by mimicking your beat, that's absolutely fine. (See upcoming chapter called "Copy Cat".)

Change roles. Squeeze yourself behind the miniature drumset. (Be careful; do not collapse the small drum throne.) Have the little one clap, stomp and respond accordingly.

If you or anyone in your family plays a musical instrument, this would be a great time to have a jam session. Play a song on another instrument and allow the young drummer to respond on the drums. Your singing voice might be the most portable instrument at your disposal. If you don't like to sing and no traditional musical instruments are available, head straight to the kitchen or garage and see what you can find that sounds good.

For example, take an empty Pringles container or pill bottle, put rice or beans inside it, and you have produced a hand-made shaker. Surround yourself on the floor with various pots and pans and play with wooden forks and spoons. Get a medium-sized box from the garage and play with it with your hands; you're now using a very inexpensive Cajon. Any puzzle boxes or Chinese Checker sets? These all make great sounds!

The Name Game

Act 1: Make sure to place the colored stickers on the drumheads, cymbals or mute pads before beginning this activity.

Sitting within striking distance of the drumset, demonstrate the colored-sticker labeling system. For instance, say the word "red" and strike the snare drum. Immediately say "red" again, but have your student play the snare drum.

***Note:** If the child wants to strike the drum more than one time, allow them to do it.*

Now play the snare drum and ask what color it is. Follow this procedure with all of the drum and cymbals and the game begins! Combine this idea with the game "Simon Says."

Act 2: The Colored Light Game–Have the young drummer pretend that the drums and cymbals are colored lights. When you say "red light," the child hits the snare drum, and when you say "green light," the child hits the floor tom, etc. Once the child gets used to the activity, proceed in rapid-fire succession.

Stick Clicking

The drumstick(s) is a great percussion tool in its own right. Sticks are very portable, easy to manipulate and produce a beautiful sound when struck together in the right way.

Act 1: To knock sticks against each other properly, hold them as if you are about to play the drums. (You may need to review a previous chapter called How to Hold the Sticks and Use the Pedal(s).) If you are right-handed, you will need to place the right stick overtop of the left stick in an "X" formation. Make sure to hold the sticks somewhat loosely and bring the right stick down to meet the left stick, making contact about 1/3 of the way down each stick (from the tip). The left stick also moves slightly upward to greet the right stick. If you desire a higher-pitched, resonant sound, have the sticks bounce off each other at contact. If you want a lower-pitched, muted sound keep the sticks together at contact.

***Note:** As always, if the student is left-handed, substitute left for right stick above.*

Act 2: The Spelling Game–Prepare by having the student write out their own name, tell you how to spell their name (and you write it out), or just write it out yourself. Do so in the following manner:

S-I-M-O-N

The dashes in between each letter symbolize stick clicks. Demonstrate how to say and play using this approach.

Your student is now ready to spell and make rhythms using other names and words.

* Then three-year-old, Simon, from the preschool at the East Valley Jewish Community Center, showed me this game in the spring of 2008.

Act 3: Counting While Clicking–First, determine how high the child can currently count. In other words, can they count from 1 to 10, 1 to 20, 1 to 50, 1 to 100, etc.? In this activity, the student clicks once at the same time as they recite each number.

One syllable numbers such as "one" and "two" are fairly easy to click and say aloud. The most natural way to execute the "teens" is the following: **thir**teen, **four**teen, **fif**teen, etc. (**twen**ty, **thir**ty, **for**ty, etc. are performed in the same way as the "teens"). However, when you arrive at 21 through 29, 31 through 39, etc., the following stick-click accompaniment makes the most sense: twenty-**one**, twenty-**two**, twenty-**three**, etc.
Demonstrate this and then have the child try counting while clicking.

Act 4: Click the Alphabet–Have the youngster click along with the syllables of the "Alphabet Song" in the following way.

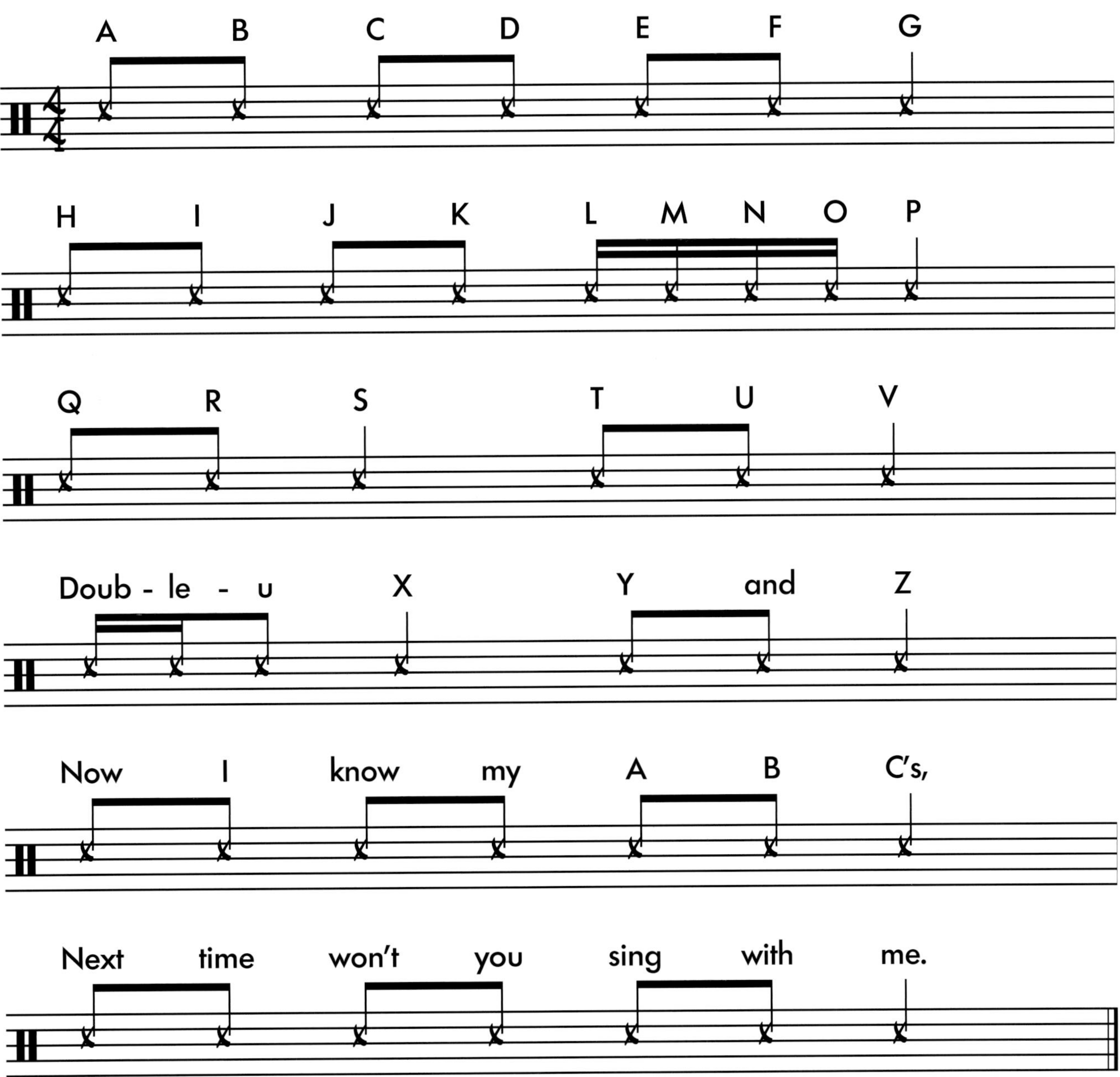

Copy Cat

One of the most effective methods for teaching drums (or any instrument for that matter) is to demonstrate a lick and have the student play it back. To the young child, this teaching technique can be especially inspiring; they perceive this as a game.

Act 1: It's time to pull out all of your extra percussion gear–see an earlier chapter called "Let's Play Together"–and set it up right next to the student kit. (You can also trade back and forth with the student on the mini-drumset.) If you happen to have an extra acoustic or electronic drumset lying around, this would be the perfect time to use it. There's nothing like performing drum duets!

Using one surface to demonstrate (ideally a snare drum), point out to the student which surface you would like them to use. If "snare drum" is not part of a shared vocabulary yet, refer to it again as the "red" drum.

Note: *Wanting to strike all of the parts of the drumset (and not just use the snare drum) is a huge temptation for youngsters. You may have to redirect the student a few times back to the snare drum.*

Play one hit on your playing surface and invite the child to copy you. Now try two hits. If the student has difficulty with this, count out "one, two" as you play. This normally clears up any confusion and the student will happily produce two hits on the snare. Continue on this manner until you get to ten snare hits. Periodically check the eyes of your student to make sure that tears are not welling up. Frustration can increase very quickly. If this happens, immediately change to a different activity or suspend drumming for the day!

Soft to Loud

Act 1: Whispering can be a challenge for young children. Practice whispering animal sounds with your student/child. Have them whisper their own names.

Once they have mastered the concept of whispering, demonstrate how to "whisper" on the drums. Explain to them that the tip of the drumstick needs to stay very close to the head. Now have the student whisper their own name (see previous chapter called "Play What You Sing"), while they play softly on the drums. Finally, allow the child to whisper their name around the entire drumset.

Tell the student to place his/her right stick on the floor tom (green) and the left stick on the snare drum (red).

Note: *If your drumset only has one or two toms, use any tom with the right stick, continuing to use the snare drum with the left stick.*

Demonstrate for the student how to play sticks one after another and at the same time. If they have trouble differentiating these concepts at this point, don't worry. Let them play on the toms any way they want to. Focusing on the concept of soft to loud is the priority at this point.

With their sticks in this position, have them play at a whispering volume and at a loud volume. Repeat this and you will soon discover a big grin on their face.

High to Low

Act 1: Using your best singing voice, glasses filled with different levels of water, a piano, or a set of orchestral bells, demonstrate notes from high to low.

Play each drum repeatedly from high to low (snare drum, high tom, middle tom, floor tom, and bass drum).

Note: *Disengage the lever on the snare drum for this activity. When a snare drum sounds more like a tom it becomes easier to hear and compare pitches.*

You will need to make sure that the drums are tuned from high to low (from snare to bass drum). It's possible to tune these drums in a number of ways. For instance, the snare drum is normally larger in diameter than the high tom. Therefore, you'll need to tune the top and bottom heads tighter than the heads of the high tom.

To check for understanding, ask the youngster, "Can you please play the highest drum?" "The lowest drum?" "The second highest drum?" And so forth...

Slow to Fast

Act 1: To tap into any prior knowledge of this topic, have your child go through the following exercise. Say your own name (first and/or last name) very slowly in an exaggerated fashion and have the student repeat it back to you. Next say your name very quickly and have them parrot that back to you. Do the same thing with the child's name. Repeat this routine with other names and words that the child knows.

Explain to the youngster that it's easier to clap slowly when you bring your hands far away from each other (after each clap). Demonstrate this. Next, explain how it's easier to clap faster if your hands are closer together. Demonstrate again. Now have the student try clapping slowly and quickly.

When playing drums, just like clapping, it is much easier to play faster when the stick height (how far the tips of the sticks come off the playing surface) stays low. In the same way, it's much easier to raise the sticks higher when playing slowly.

Act 2: Have the student place their right stick on the middle tom (blue) and their left stick on the high tom (yellow). Now encourage them to play slowly and quickly.

Finally, have the child play gradually from slow to fast and then from fast to slow.

Note: *The term "gradual" may be difficult to understand at this age range. Careful modeling of this concept may be needed.*

Drumming with Your Feet

Pop music often involves a rhythmic element called "4 on the floor". This steady beat played by the bass drum (and sometime other instruments) creates a throbbing, booming, pulsing sound that seems to infectiously cause people to dance. The type of groove is counted 1 - 2 - 3 - 4 (repeat). In other words, you count from 1 through 4 and then go back to one all over again. In the book, it's referred to as "kicking", because this technique uses only one foot at a time. Here is the drum notation for that groove.

Kicking

Act 1: Demonstrate and then have your student try this. Can they count and play at the same time?

Note: *This is a good time to review foot technique. Go to a previous chapter called "Holding the Drumsticks and Using the Pedal(s)" for a quick refresher course.*

Act 2: Both feet are used in the following patterns: "Walking" (one foot after another) and "Hopping" (both feet at the same time). Demonstrate these, and then have the child try. Again, encourage them to count while playing.

Walking

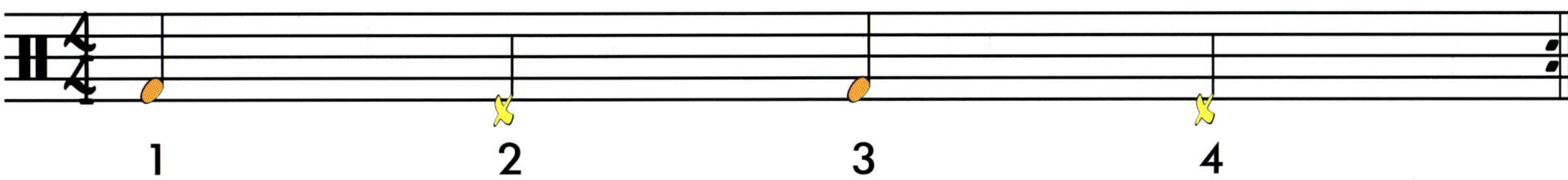

Hopping

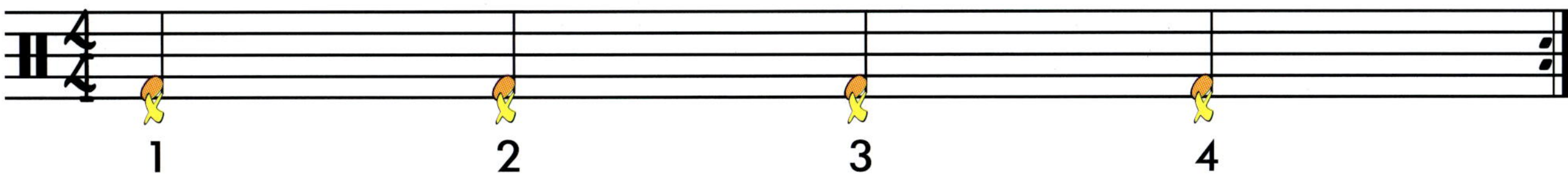

Groove to the Music

Playing beats along with recorded music or with real live musicians is one of the great pleasures of life. However, please be cautious about pushing the youngster too hard to achieve this goal. They may not quite be ready. The child's performances on previous activities in the book may clue you in on their readiness.

Find the Backbeat: Most pop songs have an easily recognizable backbeat. A backbeat is an accented note placed on beats 2 and 4 and is usually played on the snare drum. It often causes listeners/dancers to clap their hands or snap their fingers along with the music.

The backbeat in "We Will Rock You" by Queen is easily discernible. The overall beat sounds like this: "Boom-boom-bop (pause), boom-boom-bop (pause)." The "bop" sound is the backbeat.

Act 1: After pointing this beat out to the student, now clap, click your sticks, or hit the snare drum (with either stick or both sticks at the same time) along to "We Will Rock You." Try this out with different pop songs. Be careful: the drumbeats of some current day pop music avoid the use of backbeats in clever, musical ways. "Speed of Sound" and "Clocks" by Coldplay are two examples of this.

Play What You Sing

Historical Background–In locations such as Africa, New Guinea and South America, early cultures used drumming for long distance communication, often imitating spoken language. In the same way, drummers today can imitate oral language, because it is made up of syllables, the building blocks of words. For example, "cat" has one syllable and "kitten" has two syllables. Also, because words and phrases involve rhythm and inflection, drummers can simulate rests, note duration, and accents to simulate speech.

Besides emulating speech, drums (especially the drumset) do a great job of approximating melodies. Buddy Rich and Max Roach, late jazz-drumming greats, quoted nursery rhymes or well-known melodies during their drum solos. Ari Hoenig, current jazz drumming icon from New York, often uses the drums as a lead melodic instrument.

The drumset is well suited to produce melodies, because it is made up of component parts (drums and cymbals), which encompass a huge frequency range, from low to medium to high.

Act 1: Demonstrate how syllables work by using the student's own name. Der-ek would be two syllables while Mike would be only one syllable. Have the students clap or click their sticks at the same time they annunciate each syllable. Try this with the days of the week. Now try the alphabet song.

Next invite the student to play their own names, the days of the week, or the alphabet song on any one part of the drumset while they annunciate the syllables.

Count Drumula

So far in *Drumset for Preschoolers*, counting has been stressed in a "number" of ways. That type of counting (whole numbers or non-negative integers) is of course a very important staple of early childhood learning.

However, rhythmic counting is covered in this chapter. Although this type of counting uses whole numbers (1, 2, 3, and 4 for most popular music), it also involves the concept of "part of a whole" or "fraction sense."

The following method to teach rhythm has been effective with children as young as 4 years old. However, please be aware that this material may not be age-appropriate for your youngster.

If the student is able to digest this material, they will be well on their way to learning any instrument, whether it is drums, piano, guitar, violin, recorder, etc. A strong rhythmic foundation will effectively lay the groundwork for further music study.

Many cultures around the world begin rhythmic training for their children as early as the age of 3. In many cases, a system of counting rhythms out loud is taught. The cross-cultural concept is: "If you can say it, you can play it." Rhythmic training in this book also begins with counting out loud.

Note: *For more information and lessons about rhythm, check out my book, Drumcraft.*

Act 1: Have your child recite the following:

1 e + a 2 e + a 3 e + a 4 e + a

The "e" is pronounced "ee," the "+" is pronounced "and," and the "a" is pronounced "uh". In other words the student will be verbalizing the pattern in this way:

1 ee and uh 2 ee and uh 3 ee and uh 4 ee and uh (repeat back to 1)

To make sure that the space between each sound is even, use a metronome or provide for the student a human metronome by clicking your sticks producing a steady pulse.

Act 2: Once the child becomes very familiar with this rhythmic counting, now see if they can clap their hands or click their sticks while counting.

Act 3: Next, have the students play alternating strokes on the snare drum (see notation below) while counting. If they repeat this measure over and over, they will run out of breath at some point. Instruct them to inhale rhythmically during any of a's ("uh") and exhale while saying one of the numbers (1-4).

Note: *If the student doesn't seem to be able to play a note while making these unusual sounds, point to the notes as they play and count. Have the child point to each note as you play and count.*

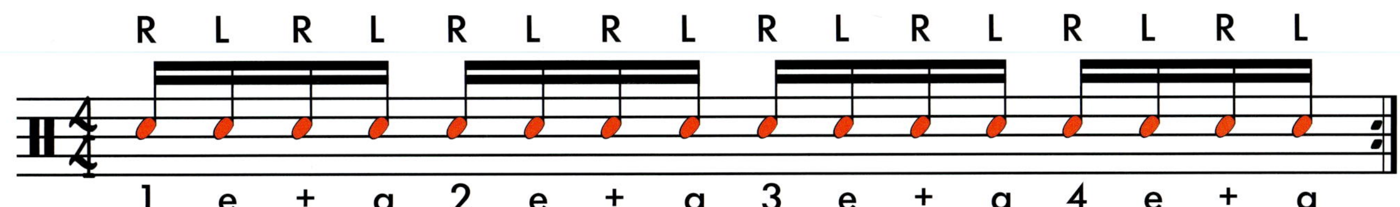

Level 2

Let's Play Together

Acquire a pair of adult-sized drumsticks from your local music store. Pull up a chair right next to the drumset near the floor tom. (If a floor tom is not available with your drumset, position yourself directly to the right of the student.)

> ***Note:*** *This is a perfect time to demonstrate proper stick or pedal technique. See "How to Hold the Drumsticks and Use the Pedals".*

Act 1: Play one side of the drumset while your student plays the other side. Switch sides and try it again. Be careful not to hit each other with the drumsticks!

Act 2: Put on some of yours or your child's favorite music, and both of you play along. Remember, in this case, it is not important to copy the note-for-note performance of the drumset artist you are listening to, only to have fun and share creativity.

The Name Game

Act 1: Play the same kind of game described in Level 1 on page 10 (The Colored Light Game), but this time, use the actual drumset vocabulary (see Drumset Diagrams). For instance, use the words floor tom, snare drum, etc., exclusively.

Act 2: Teach the vocabulary of the drumset by describing or giving background information about each component part. Below is a script of useful tidbits that might help the students remember the names of the parts of the drumset.

Snare Drum (red)–"This drum has metal strands on the bottom of it. Touch the bottom of the snare drum very gently. Look what happens when I disengage the snare strainer by moving this lever. This drum can make two different sounds! Notice when I strike the top head (with the snares on), it makes a bop sound. Bop!"

Bass Drum (orange)–"This drum is the biggest part of the drumset. It makes the lowest sound. Boom (using a low-pitched voice)! This is the only drum that you strike by using a pedal. Can you make a boom sound by using the bass drum pedal?"

> ***Note:*** *Young students often have a bit of trouble using the bass drum and hi-hat pedals at first. Read the section How to Hold the Drumsticks and Use the Pedals for further assistance.*

Hi-hat (yellow)–"The hi-hat has two cymbals that hit together and make lots of different sounds. (Demonstrate those if you have experience as a drummer.) Close your eyes. (Put the top hi-hat on top of your head.) It's called a hi-hat because it looks like a hat."

High Tom (yellow), Middle Tom (blue), and Low/Floor Tom (green)–"These are the only drums that also share a person's name, Tom. When you strike them, they sound a lot like their name." (Demonstrate by playing each tom in succession, from high to low. Then sing "tom, tom, tom", lowering the pitch of your voice as you go. If your drumset only has one or two toms, modify this approach accordingly.)

Cymbal (green)–"The cymbal makes a crash sound if you hit it hard."

Act 3: Teach the student to play the following simple patterns on the drumset using the colored-sticker system. Refer to each drum as a particular color. You might say before and/or during modeling the first line, "Red, yellow, blue, and green." The second line of music would be, "Red, red, yellow, yellow, blue, blue, green, and green." The third line would be, "Red, red, red, red, yellow, yellow, yellow, yellow, blue, blue, blue, blue, green, green, green, and green." Repeat each line as many times as possible.

Around the Drums

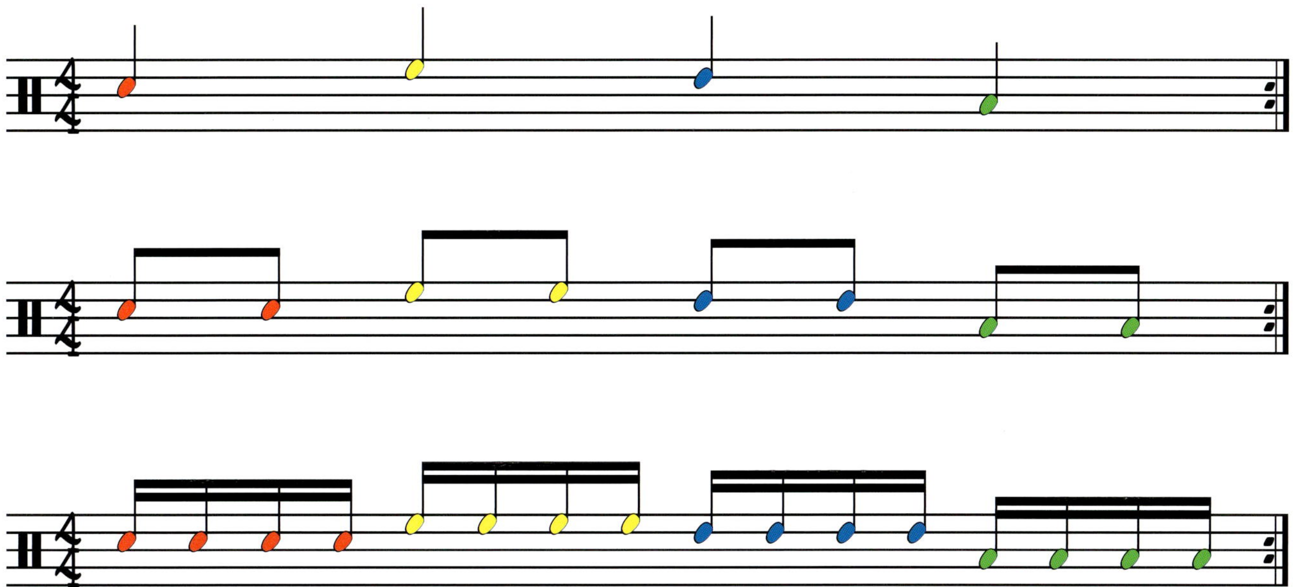

Note: *Make sure the tip of the stick bounces off the head after it makes contact, allowing the drum to resonate, instead of the tip remaining on the drumhead after contact, which muffles the drum.*

If your drumset has one tom (instead of three), double the number of hits on the snare and the tom. In other words, play twice as many of the red-labeled drums (snare) and twice as many of the blue-labeled drum (the one tom). You can also play three times as many of the blue-labeled drum (tom) and keep the snare part the same.

Act 4: Strike-the-Rim Adventure–This activity provides the student another way to learn their way around the drumkit.

Demonstrate how to hit the metal rim (rarely some rims are constructed of wood) of each drum using the neck of the stick (one to two inches from the tip). The rims can be hit on any point on the circumference, however, you may find that the portion closest to the player is easier to reach and target.

Explain to the student that you are going to play a duet together. Begin to play on the rims and have the child join you.

Note: *It's not necessary for the student to try to copy what you are playing. The goal here is simply to explore the sound of the rims of the drumset while playing together.*

Next have the student begin the rim click duet. Join in!

Stick Clicking

Act 1: "In-between-ness" is an important but oftentimes overlooked musical concept. Defined here as the placement of a note in between two notes, it explains why some rhythms sound twice as fast or half as fast as other notes.

To demonstrate this concept using stick clicking, have the student begin to click away at a slow steady rate. Place your clicks in-between each of their clicks. You'll both realize with delight that the rhythm now sounds twice as fast. Stop clicking but encourage the child to continue clicking. Now the rhythm sounds twice as slow (as the most recent rhythm). Reverse rolls and now see if the student can place their clicks in between yours.

Another way to produce the same type of alternating cooperative stick-clicking, is to first produce a single stick click. Now encourage the child to execute a click right after yours. Hit another click followed by another student click, all the while attempting to make the space/time between each click as even as possible. Continue this process as long as you can. Explain that you've been playing in a back and forth or one-after-another (alternating) manner.

Act 2: Once you and your partner have become adept at performing alternating stick clicks, try starting at a slow tempo and speed up ever so gradually. Review the concept of stick height from a previous chapter in Level 1 called Slow to Fast. Remind the student that as you increase the tempo, the stick height will decrease. As you decrease the tempo, the stick height will increase.

Perform this with your student again, but this time, go from slow to fast to slow again.

Now produce two clicks in a row and have the student respond with two clicks. Go back in forth in this manner. How about three clicks in a row?

Act 3: Click at the Same Time–Next, begin clicking in a steady manner and have the student join in with you, so that the sticks are clicking simultaneously. Click from slow to fast and from soft to loud. Reverse roles and have the student commence clicking. Try this with larger groups of people.

Act 4: Another Way to Click the Sticks–Here is truly an "alternate" method to click your sticks. Start as before, allowing your right stick to click on top of your left stick. Instead of repeating this process over and over again, this time lift your left stick up and have it come down onto your right stick. Continue in this fashion: lead with the right, then left, then right, etc.

Act 5: Stick Click Walk–Your student can learn a brand new, creative way to walk around your neighborhood. (Warning: this may elicit some strange looks from your neighbors!) Three kinds of stick click walks are detailed here.

1. Click the Sticks with Each Step–Every step is accompanied by a stick click.
2. Click the Sticks in between Each Step–Right step-click-left step-click, etc.
3. Click the Sticks While Hopping–Jump up in the air, and just as the feet make contact with the floor, click the sticks!

Note: *For tight spaces, walking in place works just as well.*

Copy Cat

Act 1: Demonstrate playing one note on each drum, from the snare drum down to the floor tom. (Refer to Around the Drums on page 17.) Now invite the student to do the same. Ideally the child should alternate strokes in this way: snare (right hand), high tom (left hand), middle tom (right hand), floor tom (left hand). If the drumset only has one or two toms, adjust accordingly.

Next, model how to play two times on each drum and have the student copy you. Again, alternate sticking leading with the right hand is the best way to go:

RL - RL - RL - RL

If it is a challenge for the child to produce two sounds on each drum, encourage them to count "one-two" as you make each hit.

Finally, have the child attempt four notes on each drum:

RLRL - RLRL - RLRL - RLRL

This time count out loud "one-two-three-four" while traveling from one drum to the next.

Act 2: When two or more parts of the drumset are played at the same time it's called a "Together Hit" or a "Flat Flam". Flams are a device used quite often in the world of percussion. The concept of together vs. separate is explored here.

Demonstrate by playing any two drums (snare, high tom, middle tom, or floor tom) at that same time. Now allow the student to try this. Continue this back and forth dialogue. The students can attempt to copy exactly what you play or can make up their own two- drum combinations.

Note: *This is a perfect opportunity to model good stick technique. Sticks should be held loosely in the hands, the pointer finger needs to stay tucked behind the stick, and the tip of the sticks should bounce cleanly off the head one time.*

Now expand this concept to playing with the feet (bass drum and hi-hat) and using the cymbals. You and your student will come up with all kinds of interesting sound combinations. You can even experiment with three sounds at once. Even four sounds at once! I don't advise trying for five sounds at once, though you could sing a note while playing!

Soft to Loud

Act 1: Play one part of the drumset softly and the next part loudly. Encourage the student to roam freely around the drums in this manner.

Act 2: Accenting is "vocal prominence or emphasis given to a particular syllable, word, or phrase" (Free Online Dictionary).

For instance, any of the syllables in the first line of "Twinkle, Twinkle, Little Star" could be accented. Try it with the child.

TWIN-kle, twinkle, little star
Twin-**KLE**, twinkle, little star
Twinkle, **TWIN**-kle, little star
Twinkle, twinkle, **LIT**-tle star
Twinkle, twinkle, lit-**TLE** star
Twinkle, twinkle, little, **STAR**

In musical terms, accenting is accomplished by playing one note louder than the others. Have the student/child play and sing "Twinkle, Twinkle Little Star" (or many others) using the same principle.

Note: *It's much easier to begin to teach this on one drum, by clapping or by clicking the sticks. Once the student has mastered accenting simple songs on one surface, then have them try to play melodically on the drumset (see Play What You Sing, Level 3).*

Act 3: In the following nursery rhyme, accenting is used. Children love to recite this and shout the word "pop."

All around the cobbler's bench
The monkey chased the weasel
The monkey thought 'twas all in fun
POP goes the weasel!

Have the student play the word "pop" on the snare drum, when it comes time to sing that word in the song.

High to Low

Act 1: The following game is a fun way to build on the pitch concept introduced in Level 1.

The High-Low Game

Materials: If possible, set up two drum kits side-by-side. If not, you will need to share one. Two pairs of drumsticks (or one shared pair) are also needed.

Instructions: One player (you for now) strikes either the high, middle or floor tom and says "lower" or "higher". The other player then strikes the drum directly higher or lower in pitch to the first drum. Now they say "lower" or "higher". The first player follows their directions and hits a drum directly higher or lower in pitch, and the game continues in this manner.

The winner of the game strikes the snare drum or bass drum the most times possible in a prescribed amount of time (Two minutes to start, but this amount of time is flexible).

After each score, the other player (not the player who struck first) needs to strike either the high, middle, or floor tom again.

Scoring: One player will be the official scorer. They will need to keep tally marks of the total number of snare and bass drum hits.

Rule: It's possible for the players to get stuck in an endless loop, hitting two or three drums (high tom and middle tom or high, middle and floor tom, for instance) over and over again. If this happens more than two times (high tom, middle tom, high tom, middle tom) the next player has to choose a different drum/direction.

Note: *You and your playing partner might soon be able to predict whether or not the person who starts the game has a huge strategic advantage.*

Slow to Fast

Oftentimes, when a young drummer is asked to play at faster tempos, they immediately tense up, gripping tightly and overuse their arms (no wrists). The following exercise will help alleviate this issue, demonstrating the importance of using a relaxed approach.

Act 1: In this workout, the right hand is placed on the middle tom (blue) and the left hand is placed on the high tom (yellow). The right hand starts the pattern and then the left hand plays in between each right stroke. Remind the child to allow the sticks to bounce off the head.

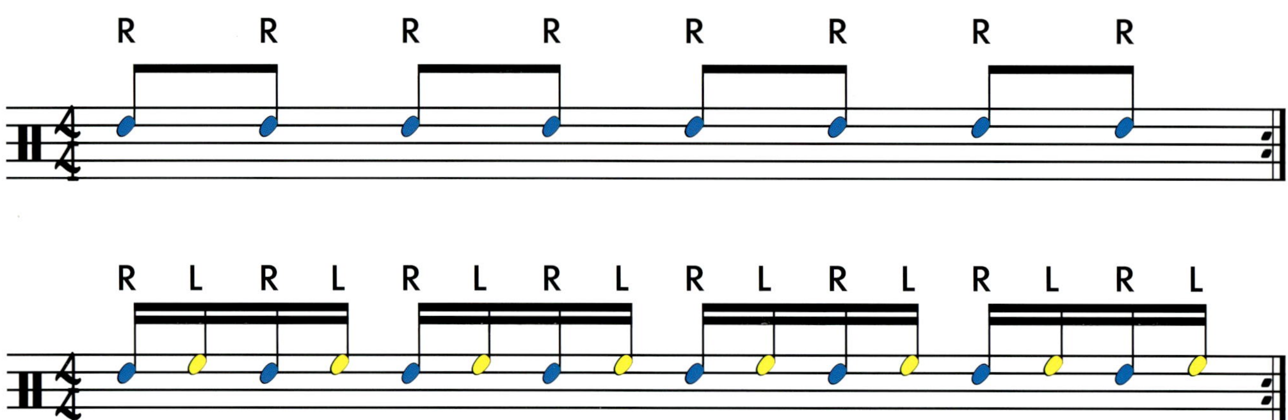

Note: *For the left-handed child, reverse the sticking. Also, if the youngster has trouble counting out exactly eight rights (high toms) in each measure, don't obsess over it. Placing a note in between another note to double the overall speed is the important concept here.*

Drumming with Your Feet

Act 1: Using the "Walking" pattern shown in Level 1, demonstrate to the youngster what this pattern sounds like a little bit faster ("Jogging") and even faster ("Running"). Now have the student try it!

Next have them play the "Kicking" and/or "Hopping" patterns from slow to fast.

Groove to the Music

"We Will Rock You" is a perfect first-time play-along opportunity. As mentioned previously, the song is recognizable to people of all ages, even preschoolers. Also, the beat itself, as performed by Roger Taylor of Queen, involves relatively easy coordination.

The following three beats can be used to play along with "We Will Rock You". The first two are grooves that sound like the actual beat, while the third one is the beat as played by Roger Taylor.

We Will Rock You (Beat 1)

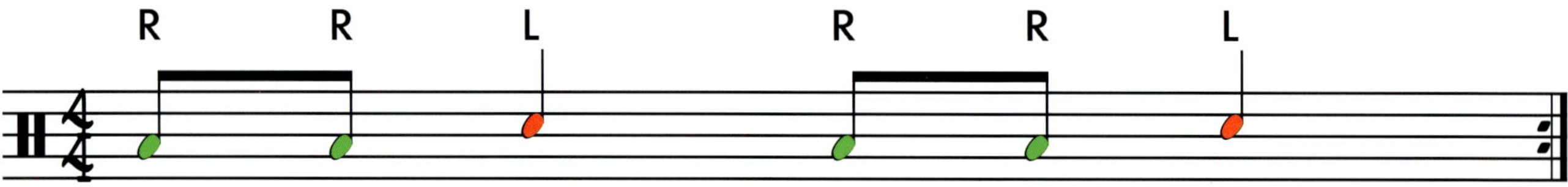

Act 1: First, tell the youngster to place their right stick on the floor tom (green) and their left stick on the snare (red). Demonstrate this pattern at a slow tempo (such as quarter note=50 bpm), saying, "Right, right, left (pause), right, right, left (pause) as you play the notes. Now have the student try it at a slow tempo. Repeat the process at or near the tempo of the song (quarter note=83 bpm). Next demonstrate the pattern while playing along with the recorded music. Now have the student try it.

We Will Rock You (Beat 2)

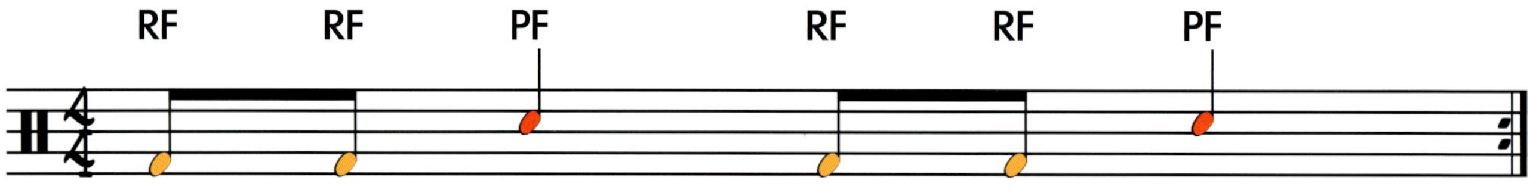

RF=right foot **PF=power flam (see explanation below)**

Act 2: The first step in teaching Beat 2 is to demonstrate how to play a "power flam". A power flam occurs when both sticks rise up to hit one drum (in this case the snare drum/red drum), but the right stick comes up slightly higher. The right stick strikes the drum slightly before the left stick, creating a thick-sounding note that fits perfectly with the Queen song.

Note: *Once the child understands how to do perform a power flam, a quick review of foot technique might also be in order (See earlier chapter called "How to Hold the Drumsticks and Use the Pedal(s)").*

Act 3: There's an old saying: " If you can say it, you can play it." Music teachers across the globe have used this concept successfully for thousands of years. The following notation shows two beatboxing possibilities for "We Will Rock You".

We Will Rock You (Beat 2 w/Beatboxing)

Either of these vocalizations could start as foot-on-the-floor and clapping hands, and then transformed into the beat shown above (with both sticks playing the snare drum and the right foot playing the bass drum pedal).

Try having the youngster play the pattern with vocalization and without. See what works the best. Now they are ready to play along with the recorded music.

There are two common challenges when young children try this groove.

1. The student's right foot tends to rise off the bass drum pedal board while playing. This is to be avoided if possible, because the ability to produce consistent bass drum hits is compromised. You may need to get on your knees and literally hold the student's foot down to the pedal as they play.
2. Because of the coordination challenges involved, the right foot may want to accidentally play on the third hit (when a power flam is the only note played by the sticks on the snare drum). To prevent this from happening, show your student how the heel of the foot (if you play with a heel-up technique) can come down and touch or almost touch the footboard in the same motion that produces the second hit. If the beater is being buried into the head (in other words, stays against the head after each hit), the child needs to then be reminded to keep their leg, ankle, and foot still during the snare drum power flam.

We Will Rock You (Beat 3)

Act 4: The groove above is the most difficult of the three beats but is probably the most fun. Power flams are played on the floor tom at the same time that the bass drum is played. Snare drum hits as power flams (followed by a pause) continue to be played as before.

The same type of coordination challenges occurs here. Three limbs (right hand, left hand, and right foot) play the first two hits, then the sticks have to strike another surface (the snare), while the bass drum remains silent at that moment. A drummer's brain finds it even more difficult than the previous beat to instruct the right foot to hold off pushing down on the bass pedal.

Once the child has this beat mastered, it's time for them to try it with the recorded music.

Play What You Sing

Act 1: Your student may be ready to sing and play a song on one surface. They may first need to learn how to sing the song, then clap their hands or click their sticks to the syllables while they sing the song, and finally sing the song while playing. The following tunes: "Bingo" and "Yankee Doodle" are notated for snare drum (red), but any surface would work.

Bingo

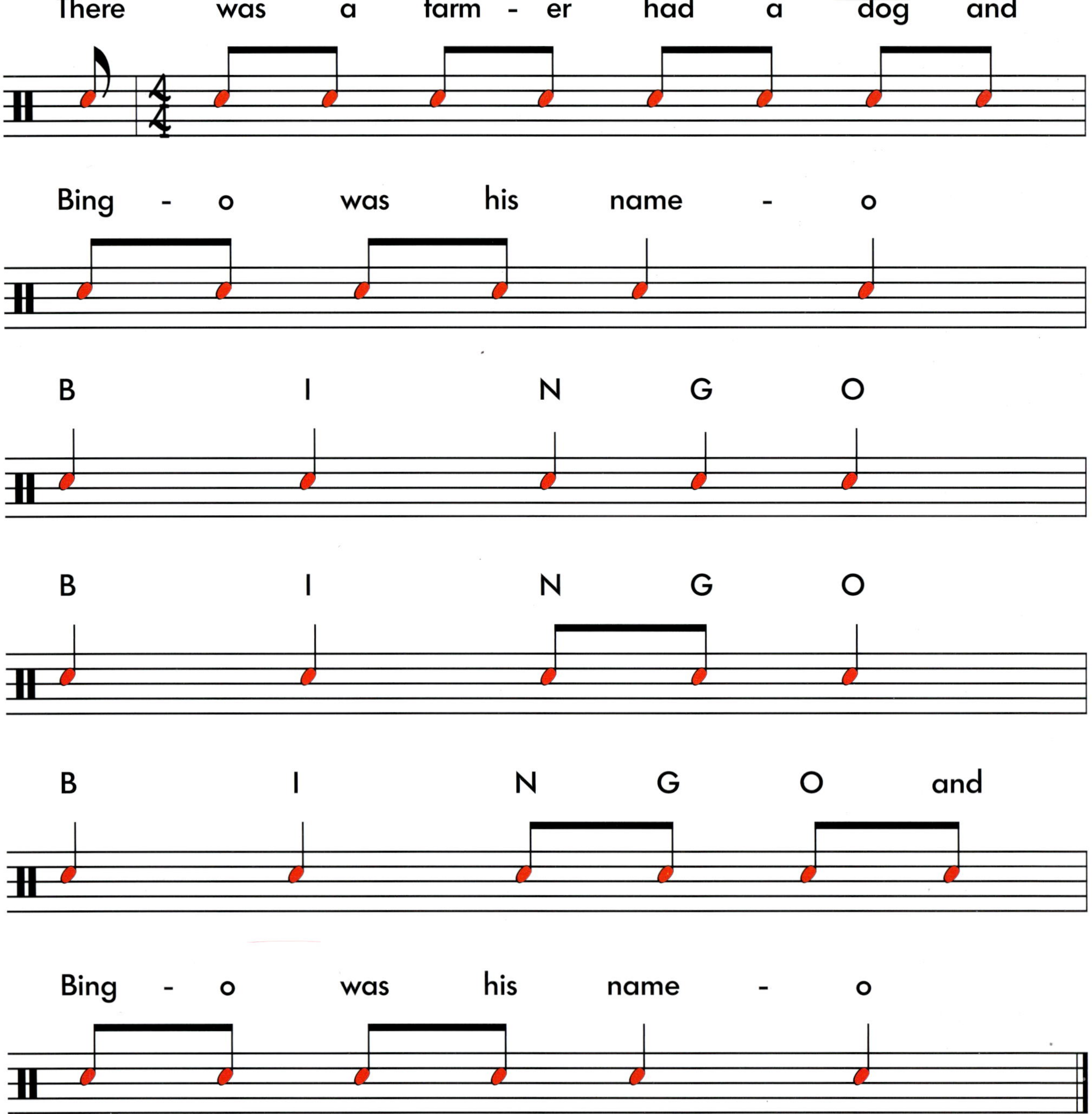

Yankee Doodle

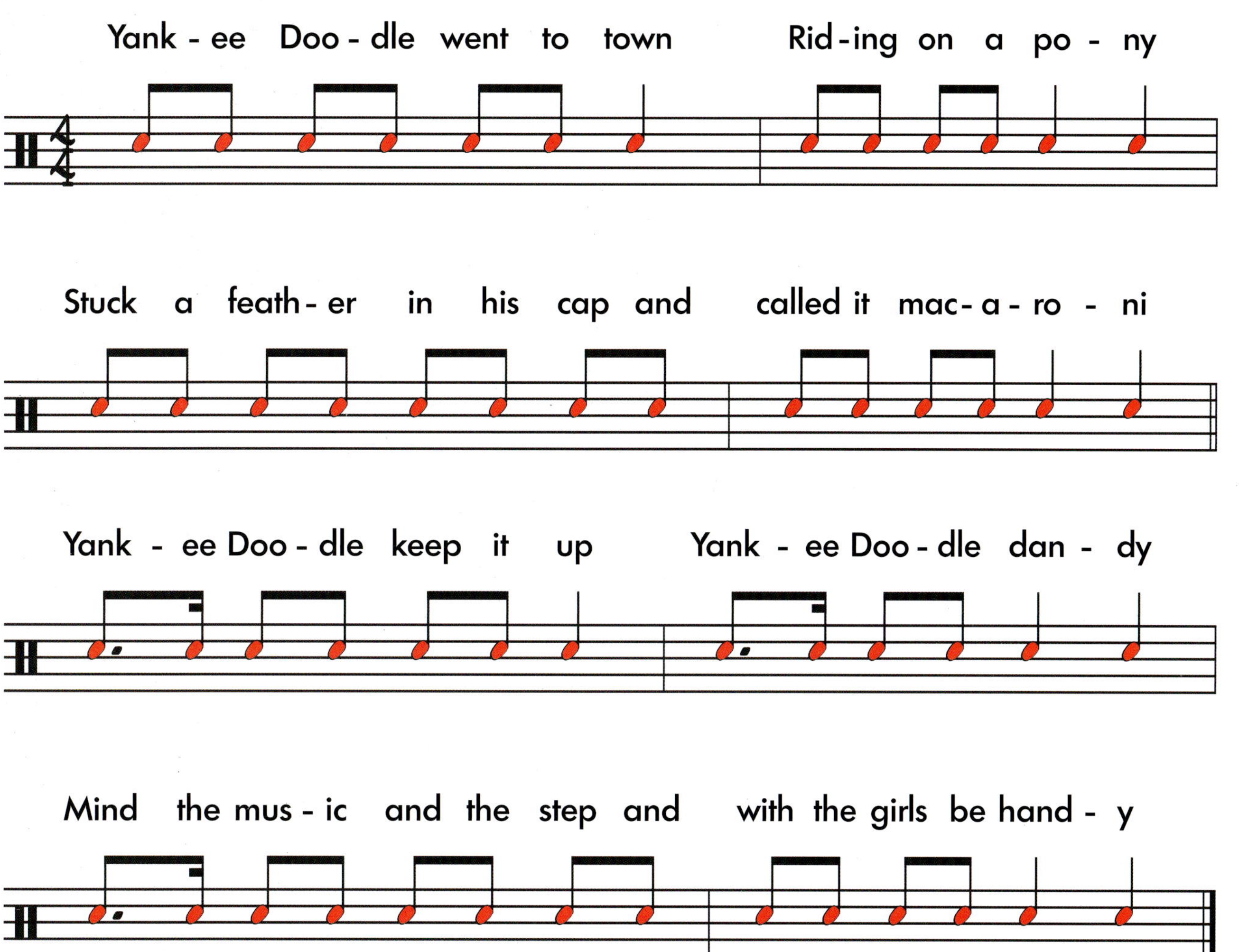

Note: *Encourage the student/child to alternate sticking (use one hand after another). However, it's not recommened that you force the child 's "hand"...*

The following list of nursery rhymes and popular songs could also be used in the same way as "Bingo" and "Yankee Doodle."

America
America the Beautiful
Baa Baa Blacksheep
Battle Hymn of the Republic
Eensy, Teensy Spider
Frosty the Snowman
God Bless America
He's Got the Whole World in His Hand
Hey Diddle Diddle
Hickory Dickory Dock
Home on the Range
Hot Cross Buns
Humpty Dumpty
I'm a Little Teapot
I've Been Working on the Railroad
If You're Happy and You Know It
It's a Small World After All
It's Raining, It's Pouring,The Old Man is Snoring
Itsy Bitsy Spider
Jack and Jill
Jack be Nimble
John Jacob Jingleheimer Schmidt
Little Bo Peep
Little Jack Horner
Little Miss Muffet
London Bridge in Falling Down
Mary Had a Little Lamb
Oh My Darling, Clementine
Pat-a-cake
Pop Goes the Weasel
Row, Row, Row Your Boat
She'll Be Coming Around the Mountain
The Farmer on the Dell
The Hokey Pokey
The Star Spangled Banner
The Twelve Days of Christmas
This Land is Your Land
This Old Man
Three Blind Mice
We Wish You a Merry Christmas
You are My Sunshine

Act 2: While playing "Bingo" or "Yankee Doodle Dandy," now invite the student to move their hands (sticks) around the drumset as they wish.

Count Drumula

Act 1: Color-coded fraction bars are a great way to demonstrate how rhythm works.

After taking a look at the chart below and reading all related information, demonstrate one measure at a time. Have your student try it! Play/count the entire chart without stopping, encouraging them to play/count with you.

Rhythm Chart in 4/4 Time (color-coded Bars)

The three following descriptions refer to one line of music notation and the corresponding color-coded fraction bar found directly underneath.

Line 1: Quarter-note (1/4 of the whole measure or bar) notation involves a notehead and a stem, but no beams attaching notes together. In the accompanying fraction bar, except for the first black line, thick purple lines (and red arrows) symbolize where the note is struck. The counting in parentheses, "e + a", is said, but not played. The counting not in parentheses, "1, 2, 3, and 4", is said and played.

Line 2: Eighth-note (1/8 of the whole measure or bar) notation involves two noteheads and stems, connected by one beam. In the accompanying fraction bar, except for the first black line, the following pattern of colored lines (and red arrows) symbolize where each note is struck: purple and pink...The counting in parentheses, "e" and "a", is said, but not played. The counting not in parentheses, "1 + 2 + 3 + 4 +", is said and played.

Line 3: Sixteenth-note (1/16 of the whole measure or bar) notation involves 4 noteheads and stems, connected by two beams. In the accompanying fraction bar, except for the first black line, the following pattern of colored lines (and red arrows) symbolize where each note is struck: purple, turquoise, pink, and turquoise. There is no counting in parentheses, because each note is said and played.

4/4: This is called a "time signature". The bottom number refers to the fact that a quarter note receives a beat. The top number refers to how many quarter notes per measure. To demonstrate this, point to each quarter note or the colored lines or arrows underneath and count, "One, two, three, four (repeat).

LCD/Subdividing: Most fourth grade math students are taught a concept called "least common denominator", which allows them to add and subtract fractions with unlike denominators. 1/4 + 1/8 + 1/16 doesn't equal 3/28. Instead, a common denominator is found between the three fractions (1/4 becomes 4/16, 1/8 becomes 2/16, and 1/16 stays the same). You can then go ahead and add the fractions together. Your answer then is 7/16!

In the same way, quarter, eighth, and sixteenth notes can more easily be counted/played together if you subdivide (a synonym for "finding the LCD") sixteenth notes. If you count and play notes as prescribed in the Rhythm Chart in 4/4 Time, you will be, in essence, providing your own metronome.

Tips:

1. Make sure all spaces between notes are equal. Playing/counting along with a metronome will guarantee a steady pulse. Also, many metronomes come with the ability to subdivide in quarter, eighths, and sixteenth notes.
2. Take advantage of the vertical presentation of the Rhythm Chart. The three measures are displayed one on top of each other. This is to show the interconnectedness between quarters, eighths, and sixteenths, even when they are not played. In other words, assuming a steady tempo and sixteenth-note subdivision throughout (counting out loud), each sixteenth-note position will be felt and heard, even when notes are not played.
3. Repeat each line as many times as necessary.
4. Point at each note or line while the student plays.
5. At first, it is wise to use incredibly slow tempos. A tempo of quarter note=20 bpm may be a good starting point.
6. Continually ask the student to identify the contents of each measure. "What are these notes called? How many eighth notes are there in a measure?"

Act 2: Arts and Crafts Rhythm Activity–Follow the steps below to give the youngster another means to help make the Rhythm Chart in 4/4 Time more concrete.

1. Fold a blank piece of white copy paper in half "hot-dog style" (the shorter side, 8.5 inches, is at the base). Fold each half in half. Finally fold each quarter in half. Unfold the paper and you should now see eight narrow bars.
2. Cut each strip of paper using the folds as a guide. You should now have eight strips of paper.
3. Use three of these strips for demonstration purposes. Three of the remaining five strips will be materials for the student, and the last two strips will be "back-up" material.
4. Fold one of your strips "hamburger style" (the longer side, 8.5 inches, is at the base) in half. Now fold each half in half and make quarters. Model this for the student and have them do the same with one of their strips.
5. Using a purple colored marker, draw lines at each fold (as shown in the Rhythm Chart in 4/4 Time, the bar that corresponds to quarter notes). Between yours and your childs sample, you should have drawn six purple lines.
6. Take another one of the blank strips and fold that strip in half, half again, and half again. You have now split the strip into eight equal pieces (eighths). Have the student repeat the process.
7. Using a pink and a purple marker, draw lines as shown in the Rhythm Chart in 4/4 Time (the bar that corresponds to eighth notes). Draw four pink and three purple lines. Have the student draw the lines on their strip.
8. Fold the last blank strip in half, half again, half again, and half again. You now should have sixteen equal pieces. The strip is split into 16ths. Have the young student follow your lead.
9. Using a turquoise, pink, and purple marker draw the bar that corresponds to sixteenth notes. In other words, draw eight turquoise lines, four pink, and three purple lines. Have the student duplicate your work.

Level 3

Let's Play Together

Act 1: Play the following patterns over and over, again, and have the child respond naturally to it.

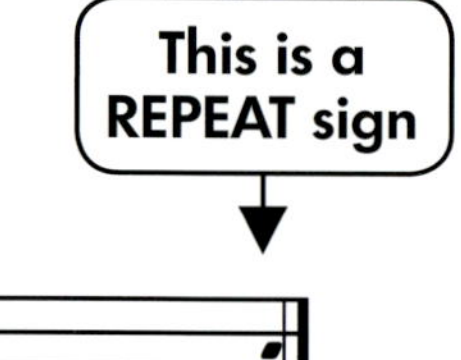

1

2

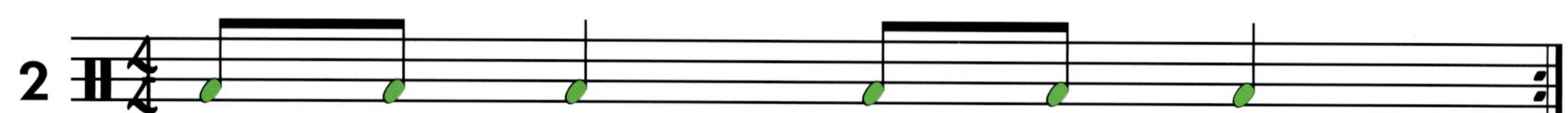

3

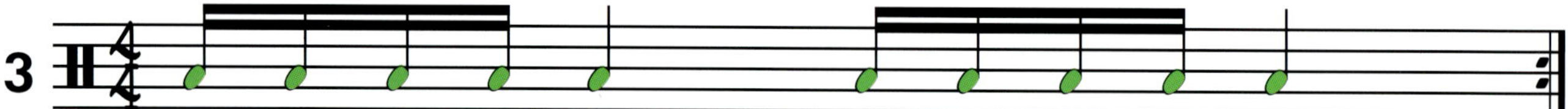

4

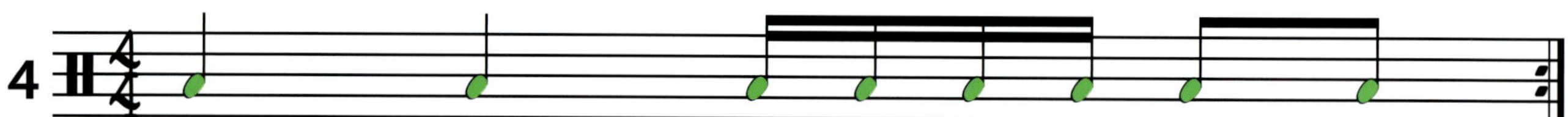

The above notation is placed on the floor tom (green) space. In this case, it is easy to position yourself behind the floor tom (alongside the child drummer), play the floor tom part as prescribed above, and allow the youngster to strike every other part of the drumkit.

Repeat these musical phrases as many times as you want.

Act 2: Now teach your student how to play each of these rhythmic patterns. Have them play the patterns repeatedly on any part of the drumset, and you can now improvise overtop of them.

The Name Game

Act 1: Tyler Tannenbaum Activity Part 1–Click your sticks in a slow, methodical manner, while at the same time, repeatedly call out "yellow". Tell the young drummer to play on the yellow-labeled drum (or point to it), the high tom, along with your clicks and vocalizations. Change colors/drums and have the youngster proceed around all the parts of the drumset.

* Then four-year-old, Tyler, from the preschool at the East Valley Jewish Community Center, created this activity in the spring of 2008.

Act 2: Tyler Tannebaum Activity Part 2–This game involves the student moving their sticks around to different parts of the drumset.

Say, " Yellow–Click–Yellow–Click" and model how to play the high tom, click the sticks, play the high tom, and click the sticks again. Try this with all of the drums and cymbals.

Now you are ready to start the game.

Call out a color and have the student play that particular drum/cymbal and then click the sticks. Have them continue doing this until you call out another color. This might cause the student to pause, recalibrate, and then start playing again. To prevent pausing, call out the colors, announcing each new color while the student is clicking. To prevent tempo fluctuations, click your sticks along with the student during the entire game.

Act 3: Now repeat the process from Act 2, but use the actual names of the drumset components.

Act 4: Sing and help play "Old MacDonald Had Some Drums" (The notation is found on the next page.) with your student.

It sometimes takes young drummers a while to get used to playing and singing. Follow these steps to help the child learn to sing/play the song. Any or all of these steps are acceptable.

1. Sit behind the drumset and play and sing the song, while the child sings along with you.
2. The child sits behind the drumset. Sing the song, while the child focuses on the drumset sounds and vocabulary. In other words, the student plays only these words and phrases: "drums", "bop-tom-tom-tom-boom", and "bop-bop."
3. The child sings the song while playing the key words detailed in # 2.
4. The child sings and plays the entire song.

"Old McDonald Had Some Drums" is written for a five-piece drumset (see Drumset Diagrams section). If you have a three- or four-piece drumset, in the "bop, tom, tom, tom, boom" line, you may need to use one or two toms, instead of three.

Note: *The names of the some of parts of the drumset, including the words "tom" and "crash" and the words used here to describe the sound of other parts of the drumset, such as "boom" and "bop" are examples of onomatopoeia. Onomatopoeia is "the naming of a thing or action by a vocal imitation of the sound associated with it" (Merriam-Webster Online Dictionary).*

Old MacDonald Had Some Drums

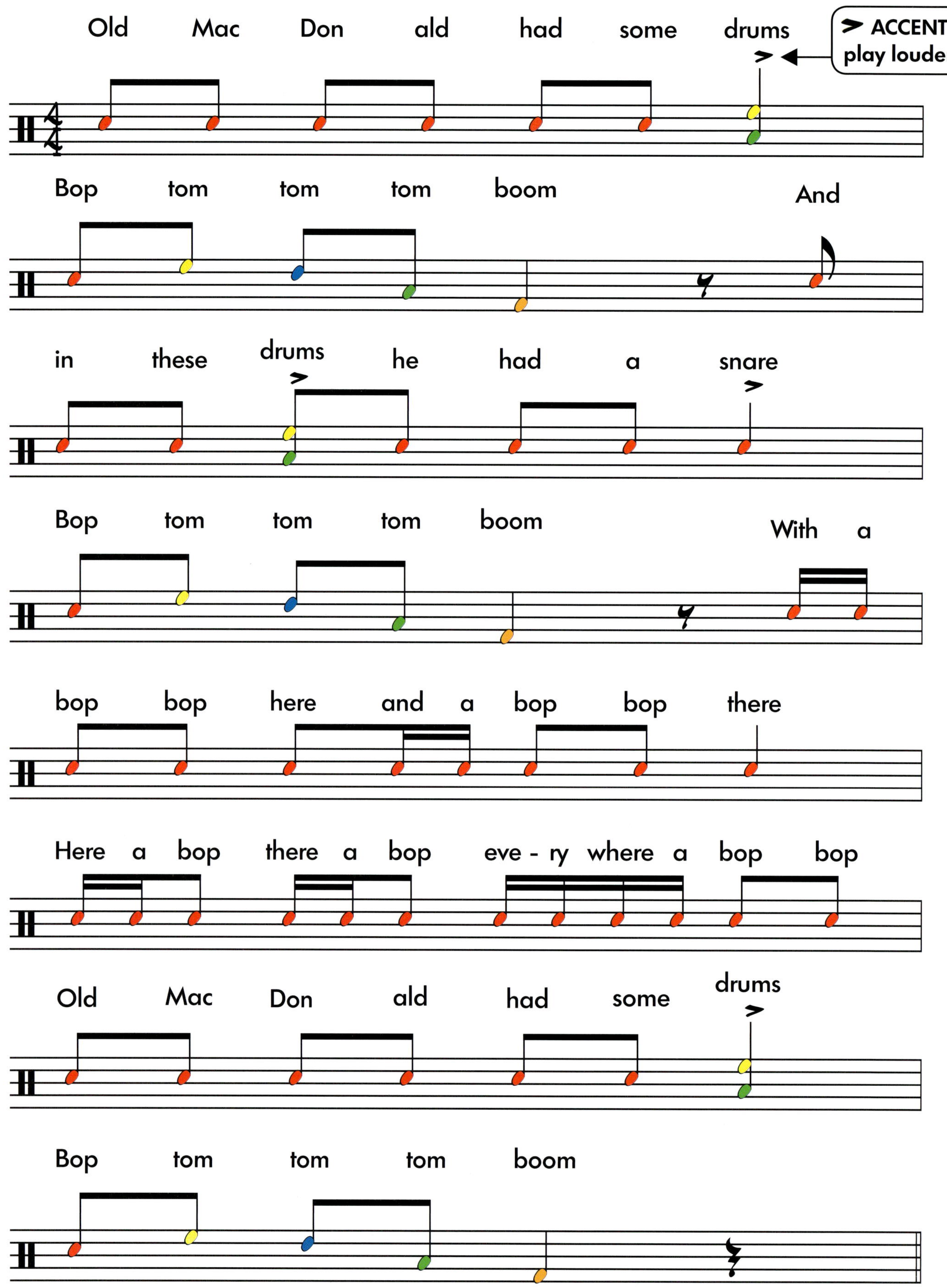

Stick Clicking

Act 1: Counting While Clicking with Partner(s)–Position yourself and two other players in an equilateral triangle. Ask the student(s) what shape you have just formed. If they are not sure, have each player hold up their arms/sticks extended straight out to the side. The triangle shape should become more obvious.

Inform the players that you will first be the leader. Click your sticks while saying "1". Motion to the next player to your left to click and say the next number. Remind the players that you are proceeding in clockwise motion. (You might want to have an clock with an old-fashioned face standing by for this opportunity.) Continue on until you reach an agreed-upon numerical goal. Change leaders. Now go in counter-clockwise motion.

Note: *For the more advanced young mathematicians, instead of counting numbers consecutively, the game is also ideal for "skip counting" (multiples) by 2s, 3s, etc. For instance: 0, 2, 4, 6, 8, etc. or 0, 3, 6, 9, 12, etc.*

Act 2: Play the same game from above, but this time use the Alphabet Song.

Act 3: Again, explore the concept of in-between-ness, but now execute one note after another (without counting out loud) in a group setting of three or more. Encourage the group to make the spaces between notes as equal as possible. If you can vary the number of players, this will demonstrate how different groupings of notes (three, four, etc.) sound/feel. Go from slow to fast and soft to loud, change leaders, and vary the clockwise vs. counterclockwise motion.

Act 4: Stomp Click Patterns–Position yourself next to the student drummer while facing away from the drumset. Using the examples below or making up your own, show the student any of the patterns and then have them copy you. Once they get the hang of it, the student can then be the leader. If the patterns cause confusion of frustration, try slowing then down.

Copy Cat

Act 1: Again playing on one surface (the snare drum, in this case), play the following short, recognizable rhythms and have the student play them back. Feel free to make up your own rhythmic phrases.

Note: *If the child has difficulty copying you, try playing the passages at slower tempos.*

Act 2: The following exercise reverses "Around the Drums," mentioned in Level 2 of this chapter. Demonstrate this exercise to the youngster in the same way, but attempt to have him/her use the following sticking patterns:

L – R – L – R : one note per drum

L R – L R – L R – L R : two notes per drum

L R L R – L R L R – L R L R – L R L R : four notes per drum

Around the Drums (Reversed)

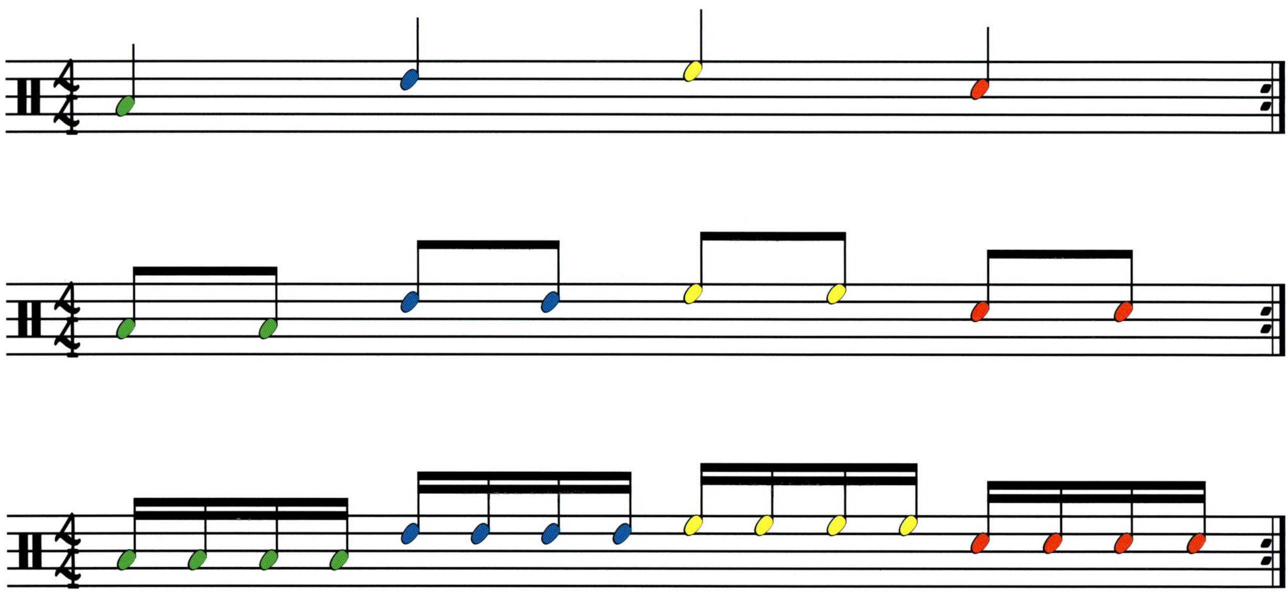

Act 3: In the next set of exercises, the hands (sticks) move from the snare drum down to the floor tom, but the right foot (bass drum) is also used. Let's see how well the cat can copy you!

Hand-Foot (Bass Drum)

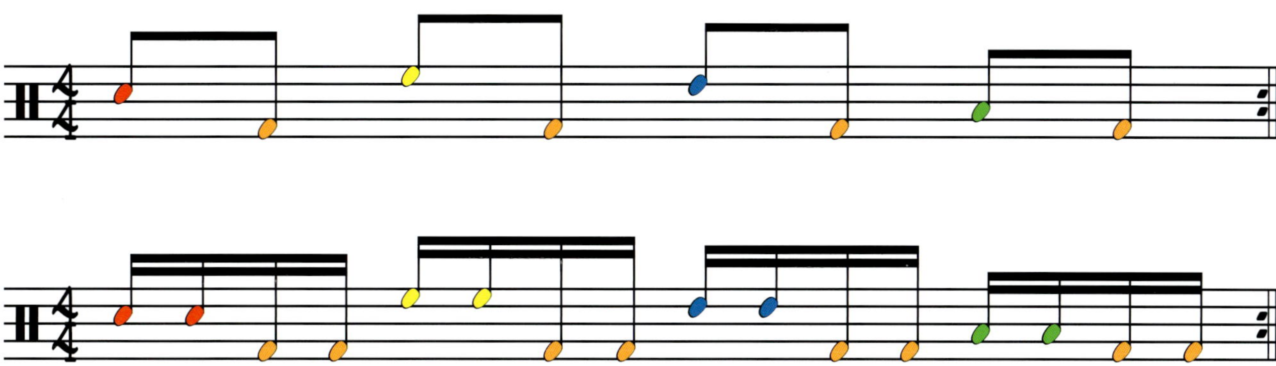

Note: Hi-hat chicks with the foot could be substituted for bass drum hits in the above exercise.

Foot-Hand (Bass Drum)

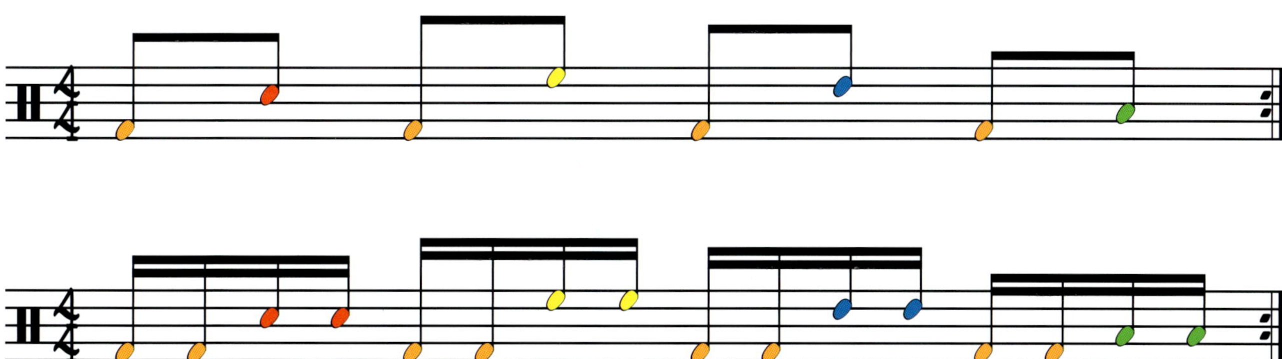

Note: Again, hi-hat chicks could be substituted for bass drum hits.

Soft to Loud

Act 1: A crescendo is a musical phrase with gradually increasing volume. Children can have a great time learning this concept.

Repeat a word over and over, starting very softly and gradually becoming louder and louder. Encourage the child to copy you.

Next, ask the student to play the same word on the snare drum, starting with a whisper and gradually increasing the volume until the word is as loud as it can go. They have now played a crescendo.

Act 2: Have the child place their right hand on the floor tom (green) and the left hand on the snare (red) and play from soft to loud as shown in the first line of notation below.

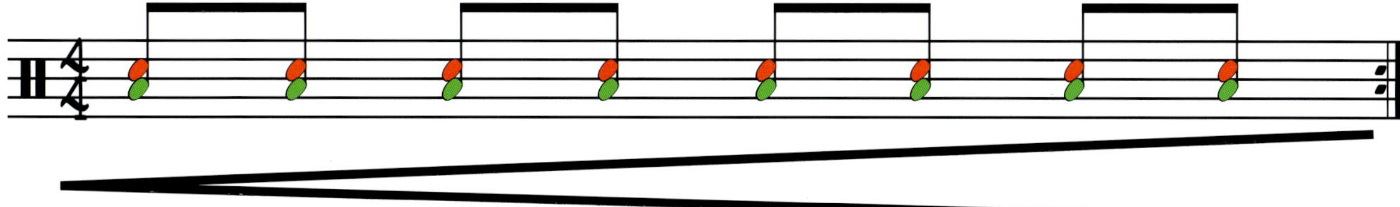

Note: The "less than sign" that you see above is music notation for crescendo.

Finally have the student place their right hand on the middle tom (blue) and their left hand on the high tom (yellow), as shown below and perform this crescendo.

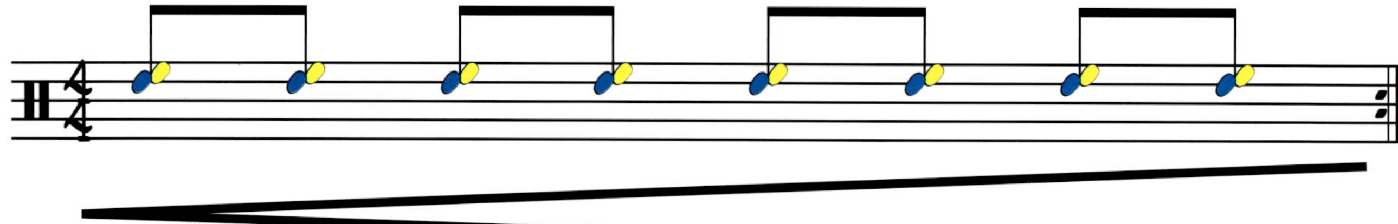

Act 3: Songs such as "Yankee Doodle" and "Bingo" are both excellent for singing softly and loudly. Now, as described in the Play What You Sing chapter (level 2), ask the student to play and sing one of these songs. But this time, invite them to sing/play part of the song softly and another part loudly.

High to Low

Act 1: The following pattern is a great way to master the concept of higher/lower pitched drums.

The most efficient way to proceed is to follow the sticking shown above the drum notation. RF=Right Foot.

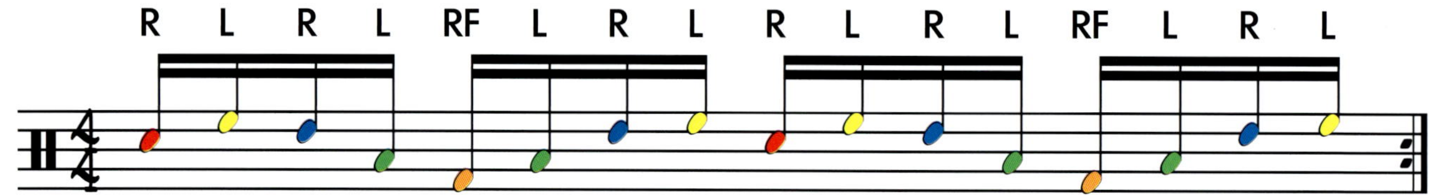

Slow to Fast

Drummers often go completely wild at the end of song before finishing with one loud bang. Recently (because of the video game, *Rock Band*) this has become known as a "big ending". If you can find any audio or video example of this, it would be helpful. Explain to the student that you are going to show them one way of producing a big ending.

Act 1: Have the student choose one of the drums (snare, high tom, middle tom, or floor tom). Using alternate sticking (one hand after another), encourage the youngster to play from slow to fast or from fast to slow.

Act 2: Next have the child hit the cymbal (green) with their right stick and the bass drum (orange) with their right foot at the same time.

> ***Note:*** *To get a crash sound, the shoulder/shank of the stick (a few inches from the tip) strikes the side of the edge of the cymbal.*

Once they learn this skill, the student may want to produce this sound repeatedly (Make sure that ear plugs or mute pads are handy!).

Here is what that ear-splitting exercise of crash hits looks like:

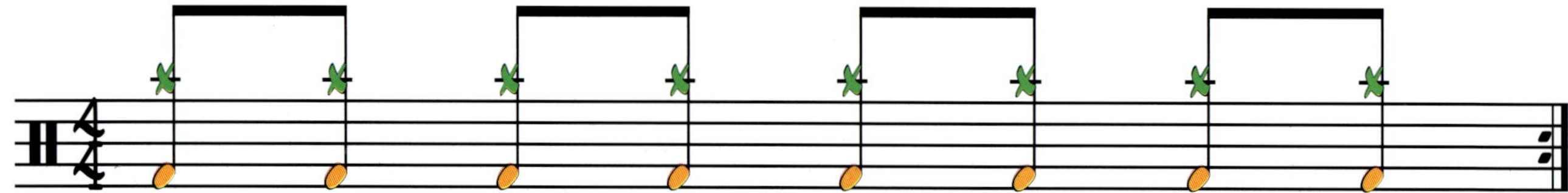

Act 3: Linking the two previous skills produces the desired "big ending": drumming on one surface from fast to slow or slow to fast, followed by one loud cymbal crash (with bass drum hit).

Act 4: Now that the student has experience playing from slow to fast on one drum, it's time to try this concept on multiple surfaces.

Demonstrate slow alternate strokes on one drum and then have the sticks travel to another drum. (You can skip around from drum to drum, instead of moving from high to low or low to high). Explain to the child that your eyes move to the next drum and target the center of that drum before the hands move. Have them try it.

Finally, demonstrate playing in this way at faster and faster tempos. Have the student try this.

Note: *Moving from one drum to the next is made easier by knowing which hand is about to travel to the next drum. Assuming that the student plays alternating strokes, an even number of hits on each drum (two, four, six, or eight) will achieve the best result. Using an even number, the child will start with his/her right on one drum and then travel to the next drum also using the right hand.*

Drumming with Your Feet

Act 1: Put on your favorite pop song that uses "4 on the floor". Below is an extremely short list of songs that use this pulsating groove:

Another One Bites the Dust	Queen
Blue Monday	New Order
Celebration	Kool and the Gang
Eye of the Tiger	Survivor
Heart of Glass	Blondie
Holiday	Madonna
I Will Survive	Gloria Gaynor
Last Dance	Donna Summer
Life During Wartime	Talking Heads
Satisfaction	Rolling Stones
Starlight	Muse
Stayin' Alive	Bee Gees

Demonstrate the "Kicking" bass drum pattern from Level 1 while the music is playing. Now have the student try it.

Next have the student perform "Walking" and "Hopping" along to the "four on the floor" dance music.

Groove to the Music

Act 1: There are generally two ways to take existing rock beats and make them easier to play, but still make them groove well with the music.

To visualize how this is done, first take a look at the following common rock beat.

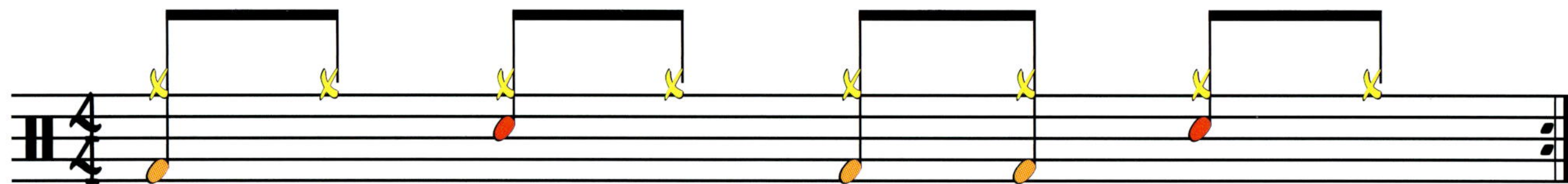

1. Ease coordination

a. Keep the bottom–sacrificing the high frequency sound of the hi-hat.

i. Floor tom and snare–the floor tom replaces the bass drum.

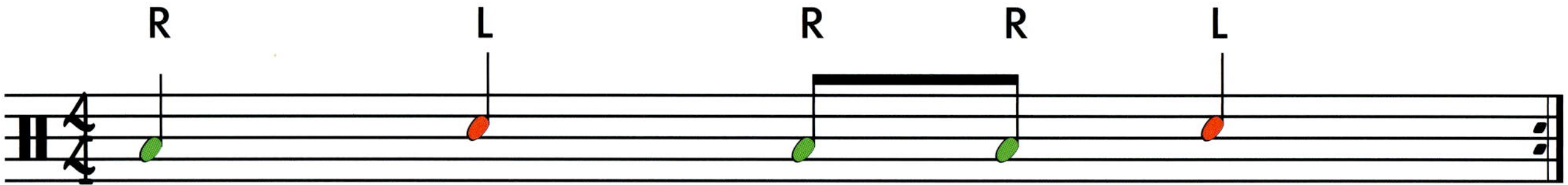

ii. Bass drum and snare

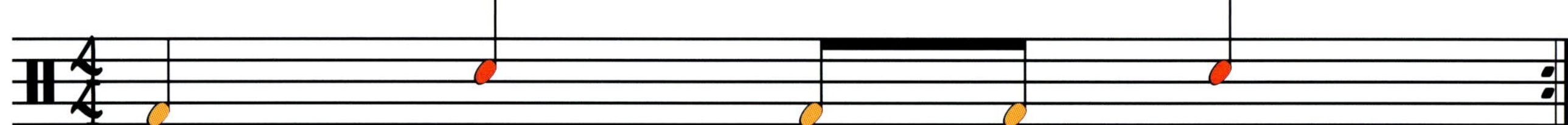

b. Keep the top–the high frequency sound, sacrificing the rhythmic content of the bass drum.

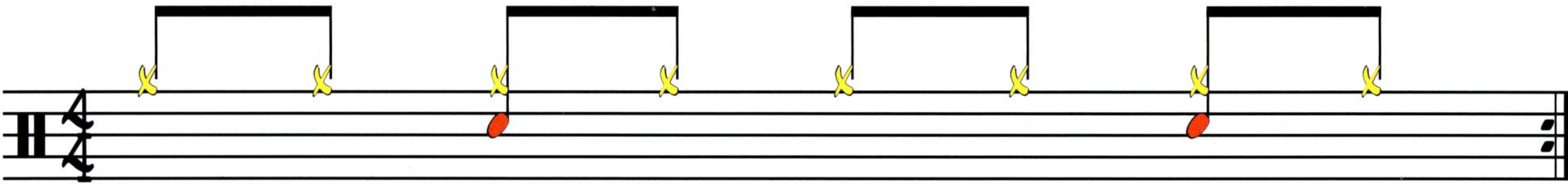

2. Simplify or delete rhythmic content:

c. Reduction in bass drum hits (In this case, the third bass note was deleted.).

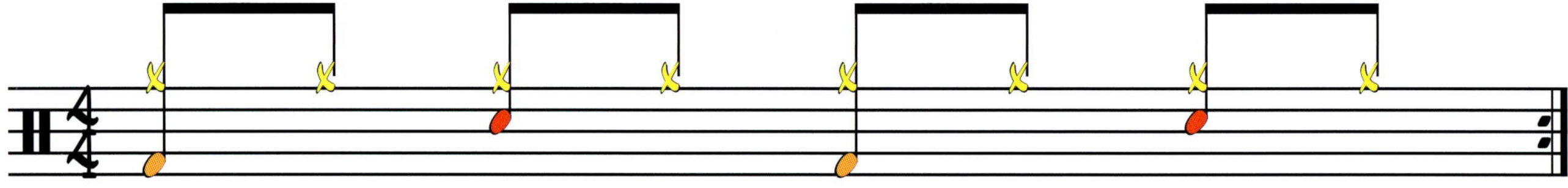

d. Reduction in hi-hat notes (All of the off-beats are taken away from the previous beat.).

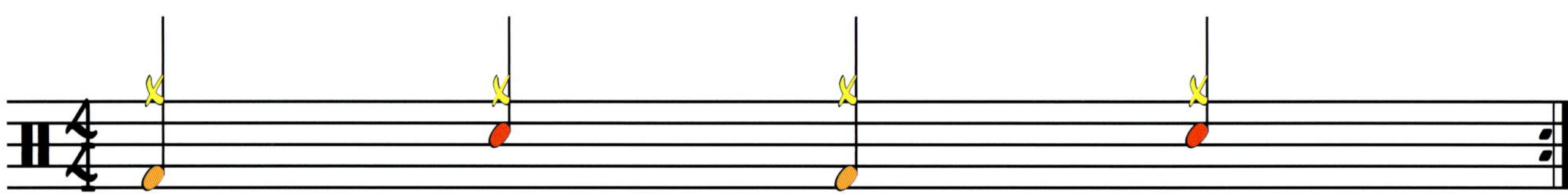

Note: *Be careful on this one. If the off-beats were taken out of the original beat, the coordination actually becomes much more difficult.*

Some young people are ready to play along with recorded music (or with live musicians) at a very young age. Others have trouble conceptualizing what it means to play along with a recording. Sometimes the sound of the music itself can cause a huge distraction.

Here are a few suggestions on how to help facilitate the play-along process. Remember to not push the young student on this. Given another 1-3 years of brain development (and the ability to handle more abstractions), almost all children can accomplish this feat.

1. As I've repeatedly mentioned in the book, demonstrating drum patterns to the youngster–and having them play it back for you–is the most sure-fired way to go.
2. Encourage the student to stop if they get lost in the music, find beat 1 again (most often beat 1 is a bass drum/hi-hat hit), and then resume grooving.
3. Have the student listen to the music repeatedly without playing (or singing/talking). This will give the young drummer time to become acclimated to their musical surroundings.
4. Play the game "Find the Backbeat" found earlier in Level 1.
5. Have the child learn the lyrics and sing along to the song. Oftentimes, drumming goes hand-in-hand with the rhythm of the lead vocal melody. Increased awareness of the vocal line will make performing the drum accompaniment much easier. It gives the young drummer a better idea when they are out of sync with the music.

If you like the idea of using rock or pop music to inspire young children, but would rather avoid some of the adult lyrical content, here is a highly recommended list of music designed for children.

A Family Album	The Verve Pipe
All Recordings by	Imagination Movers
All Recordings by	The Wiggles
Choo Choo Soul	Choo Choo Soul
For the Kids	Nettwerk Records (various artists)
Hey You Kids	The Jellydots
Music Play Date	Playhouse Disney (various artists)
No!	They Might Be Giants
Records Produced by	Kids Bop (kid-friendly versions of the latest songs on Top 40 radio and are sung by kids for kids)
Snacktime!	Barenaked Ladies

Note: *Contact a private drum instructor for assistance or information on transcription tools such websites, software, and books.*

Play What You Sing

Refer to the previous section, How to Set Up and Tune a Drumset, for tuning tips.

Act 1: Teach your student/child to play the approximate rhythmic melodies of "Jingle Bells" found below. Once they become comfortable playing the piece, see if they can sing and play the song at the same time.

Jingle Bells

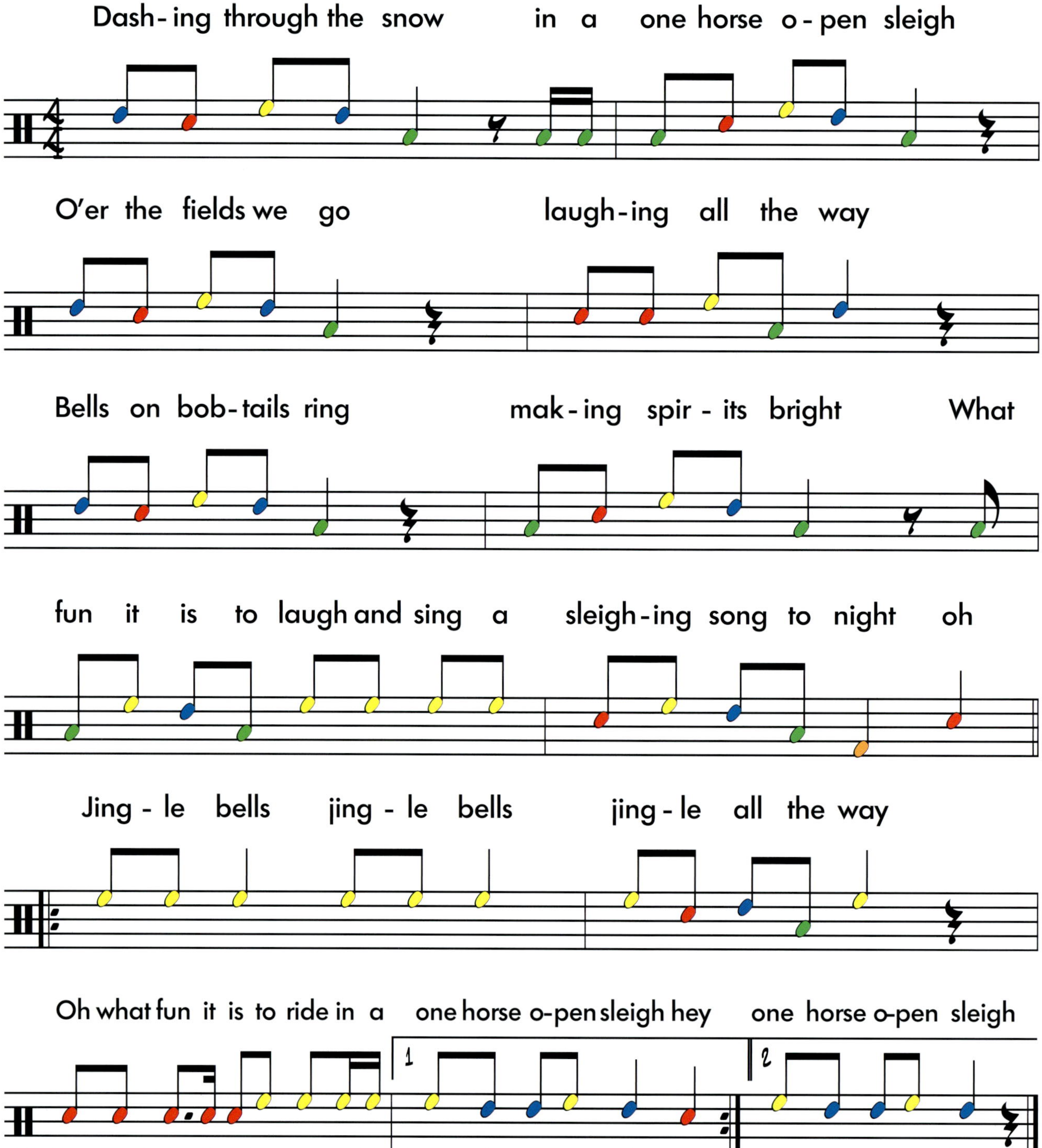

The following two songs: "*Oh Susanna (Drummer Version)*" and "*Twinkle, Twinkle, Little Drum*" use the same concept as the tunes shown on pages 22 & 23. However, in this case, the words have been changed to accommodate a drumming theme and more drums are used to highlight the shape of the melody.

Oh Susanna (Drummer Version)

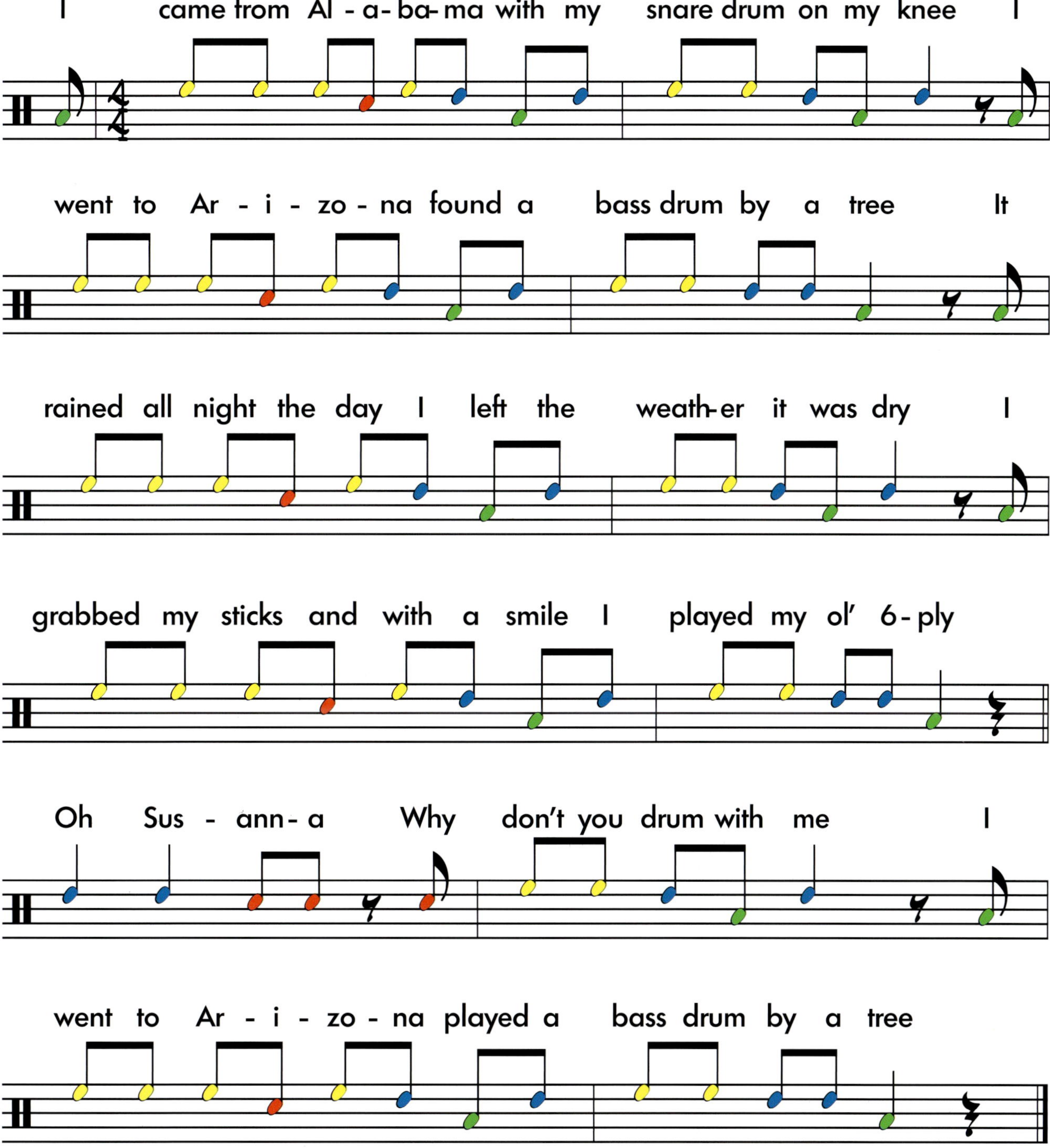

Twinkle, Twinkle, Little Drum

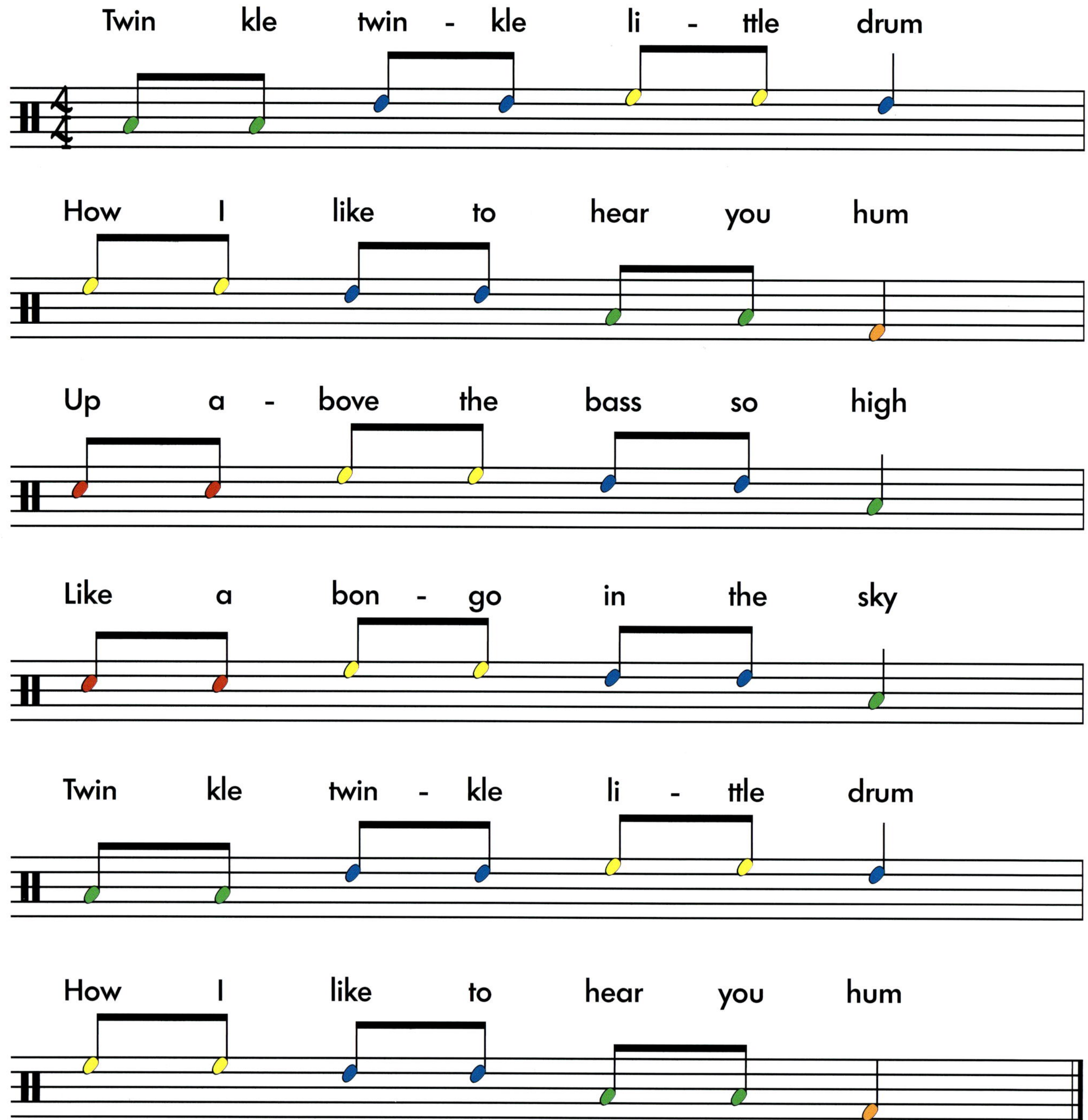

Note: *Using the last two songs as examples, you might want to work with your child to change the words (you could use any of the songs listed on page 23) but keep the syllables (rhythm) and melody the same. This can be a rich vocabulary-building and musical experience for your child.*

Count Drumula

Act 1: Play "Around the Drums" from an earlier chapter called The Name Game and "Around the Drums (Reversed) from an earlier chapter called Copy Cat. This time, while playing these exercises, count using a sixteenth-note subdivision (LCD).

Act 2: In this culminating activity, quarter, eighth, and sixteenth notes are played all within one rhythmic piece. Sixteenth note-subdivisions are provided to aid in counting while playing.

The following piece is notated on the snare (red) space, but any one drum or combinations of drums/cymbals could be used.

The Kite

Conclusion

Congratulations, whether or not your child was able to get through all of the material in this book, you have definitely extended the life of your mini-drumset (or electronic device, etc.) and hopefully provided them with a valuable learning experience. If your student really enjoyed the *Drumset for Preschoolers* adventure, and you think they are ready for more, the following insight might be helpful.

1. The general music skills covered in *Drumset for Preschoolers* provide a great foundation to learn any instrument. How do you go about picking an instrument for the young student?

   I would recommend playing recorded music or going to see live concerts with the child. Make sure that the music covers a wide range of genres and uses a multitude of instruments. Go to a music store and have the employees demo a number of instruments. Find out if the music store sponsors recitals for their music students. Go to one or more of these recitals as a spectator. Observe the reaction of your child, and after a short period of time, the answer should become obvious.

2. If you'd like to go forward with drumset as a primary instrument, you might be interested in another one of my books called *Drumcraft. Drumcraft* starts where *Drumset for Preschoolers* leaves off.

3. If you haven't done so already, seek out a private instructor for your child. The kind of one on one attention and expertise that the youngster will receive cannot be matched.

4. Continue playing the games and exercises found in *Drumset for Preschoolers.* Review is one of the most powerful tools of teaching/learning.

5. When your child reaches the appropriate age, make sure to enroll them in their school's band program (unless the school doesn't have one).

6. As I mentioned in the introduction, music related video games such as *Rock Band* can provide key motivation to get your child to want to learn a real instrument.
   If you visit my website, www.andyziker.com, you'll find a tool designed to turn gamers into drummers.

7. Learn a musical instrument yourself. When your child sees your dedicated effort, they may follow suit.

8. Once your child has outgrown the mini-drumset, instead of throwing it away, gift it to a preschool or a neighborhood family. You might even be able recommend a certain book to them!

About the Author

Andy Ziker is a 29-year drumming veteran. During a trip to New Orleans at 13 years old, Andy was so impressed with the rich musical atmosphere of Bourbon Street and a one-man-band street musician playing a set of junk drums that he began taking drum lessons on his first drumset, an old pieced-together Slingerland. When a neighborhood friend wanted to form a heavy metal group, the band Zarcus was born

Andy played in a number of bands while studying with Billy "Stix" Nicks, a brilliant drum instructor in the South Bend area. His musical momentum flourished with the continuous support of his dad, as he performed diverse musical styles including rock, new wave, blues, jazz, Latin, and pop rock. He improved his music theory and orchestral percussion skills in order to enroll in the music program at Arizona State University (where he studied with Rob Schuh and Dom Moio), and graduated with a degree in music in 1991. Andy also had the thrill of studying with drumming guru Don Bothwell at that time.

Along the way, he began teaching drum lessons at Linton-Milano Music in Mesa, Arizona.
He earned a master's degree in Elementary Education in 1995. He continued to play freelancing drum gigs around town, while teaching fourth graders for five years, and middle school science for one year. Drum teaching has remained a constant in his life for more than 20 years. Studying drumming has led Andy to connect with numerous mentors such as Jeff Hamilton, Colin Bailey, and Dom Famularo. Thanks to funding from the Arizona Commission on the Arts grant program, he has expanded his training to include one-week visits to New York City with John Riley.

Recently Andy has published articles in Modern Drummer, Drummer Café, Online Drummer, and Percussion Partners websites, and the Destructoid blog. He also established a Preschool Drumset Program at the Barness East Valley Jewish Community Center in Chandler, Arizona. He has published four other drum instructional books: *Drumscapes* (self-published), *Drumcraft* (Cherry Lane Music Company), *Drum Aerobics* and *Daily Drum Warm-Ups* (*Hal Leonard*). Besides working as a freelance musician, Andy is currently playing with eight music groups: Dave Henning 4, Avalon, the New Westerns, the Tommy Eggleston Trio, NuWorld Jazz Project, Stan Sorenson and Jazz Prose, Stevie Ray and the Allnighters, and Jed's a Millionaire. He also teaches two percussion classes at Self Development Charter School in Mesa, AZ.

Andy is available for session work, private lessons (including Skype lessons), clinics and workshops. He endorses TJS Custom Drums and Aquarian Drumheads and is a member of Jazz in AZ, Percussion Partners, and the Percussive Arts Society.

For more information about the author, free video content that accompanies this book and *Drum Aerobics*, and other percussion nuggets, go to www.andyziker.com. Andy can also be found on Facebook, MySpace, Linkedin and Twitter.

Acknowledgements

TRY Publishing for this opportunity
my wife Cindy for her constant support and understanding
my entire family for their encouragement
Lisa Webb from Southwest Shots Photography
Will Palmer for his mastery of the English language
all of the young drumming models
Jo Ramirez for her illustrations
Jackie Silberg for showing the way
Don Bothwell
Billy Stix Nicks
John Riley
Rob Schuh
Dom Moio
the Kyrene School District
Arizona State University for their instruction and training
Bart Elliott
David Stanoch
Tom Morgan
Dan Brigstock
Mike Dolbear
Michael Brucher
Roy Burns
Chris Brady
Dave Heim
Matthew Self
Todd Norris
Rick Schiller
Dave Baradic
Tom Schultz
Dave Black
Jeff Schroedl
Nate Brown
Ludwig Drums
Zildjian Cymbals
TJS Custom Drums
Aquarian Drumheads
Percussion Partners
Drummer Café
OnlineDrummer.com
Virtual Drummer School
Modern Drummer Magazine
the Percussive Arts Society
Jazz in AZ
Milano Music

all of my drum students (especially in this case, the young ones) and their parents
for allowing me to learn as I teach

and especially the students, teachers, and administrators
at the Barness East Valley Jewish Community Center Preschool

I'd also like to thank all of the musicians and educators who have influenced me throughout the years.

Other Books Available from TRY Publishing

Independence for the Beginner Vol 1

Great beginning Jazz Be-Bop book. Works with the "jazz ride beat" and helps develop flexibility with your hand foot coordination. This book progresses at a comfortable pace for better comprehension.

Independence for the Beginner Vol 2

This book takes the "jazz ride beat" up a notch from Volume 1 and further develops flexibility improving hand foot coordination on the drum set.

Developing Dexterity for Snare Drum

A collection of stick exercises to aid the snare drummer in developing a strong technical foundation. Includes exercises covering single strokes, rolls, flams, paradiddles, rebound strokes, buzz strokes, and other aspects of snare drum technique.

Elementary Snare Drum Studies

A well balanced collection of basic studies in reading and technique, intended to provide the beginning drummer with a strong foundation in the essential fundamentals of drumming.

Intermediate Snare Drum Studies

A collection of 43 intermediate studies for snare drum in two parts. Part one emphasizes basic techniques: Part two is a collection of studies with emphasis on dynamics, phrasing, and control.

Advanced Snare Drum Studies

A collection of advanced studies for snare drum, with emphasis on control, touch, phrasing and style.

Rudimental Primer

Intended to provide the drummer with a solid foundation in the traditional rudiments. Each rudiment is presented in its basic form followed by short, related patterns and exercises which focus on the technical demands of each rudiment.

Odd Meter Rudimental Etudes for Snare Drum

A long overdue and comprehensive collection of stick exercises for the snare drummer. All exercises are in unusual time signatures. This book is of benefit to the student or the professional.

Odd Meter Calisthenics for the Snare Drummer

A long overdue and comprehensive collection of stick exercises for the snare drummer. All exercises are in unusual time signatures. This book is of benefit to the student or the professional.

Funkacises

Funk and Rock exercises from beginning to advanced. Funkacises helps the development of 4-way coordination from the drum set and contains over 40 different beats and patterns for the rock drummer.

Musicians Guide to Chord Progressions

In this book you'll learn how to: Learn chords and progressions by the use of chord charts; Teach application of the chords to songs (melody lines); Develop relative pitch; Give examples of chording (comping) behind a soloist; And give examples of rock music chording.

ChopBuilders

Take your technique to boot camp! Great "woodshedding" book that helps develop snare drum technique with the use of the three basic rudiments, single stroke roll, double stroke roll, and the flam.

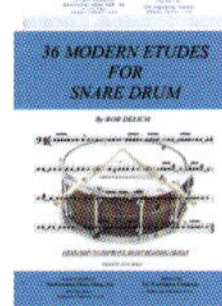

36 Modern Etudes For Snare Drum

Designed to give the drummer reading material in time signatures not commonly seen. Besides cut time, which in itself is useful, the exercises are presented in 5/2, 9/2, and 11/2 among others. These exercises are not pattern based, they are rhythmic compositions offering a real world reading challenge making them ideal for the drummer seeking to improve their sight reading.